Fists and Flowers
A Social Psychological
Interpretation of Student Dissent

SOCIAL PSYCHOLOGY

A series of monographs, treatises, and texts

EDITORS

LEON FESTINGER AND STANLEY SCHACHTER

Jack W. Brehm, A Theory of Psychological Reactance. 1966

Ralph L. Rosnow and Edward J. Robinson (Eds.), Experiments in Persuasion. 1967

Jonathan L. Freedman and Anthony N. Doob,
Deviancy: The Psychology of Being Different. 1968

Paul G. Swingle (Ed.), Experiments in Social Psychology. 1968, 1969

E. Earl Baughman and W. Grant Dahlstrom, Negro and White Children:
A Psychological Study in the Rural South. 1968

Anthony G. Greenwald, Timothy C. Brock, and Thomas M. Ostrom (Eds.),
Psychological Foundations of Attitudes. 1968

Robert Rosenthal and Ralph Rosnow (Eds.), Artifact in Behavioral Research. 1969

R. A. Hoppe, E. C. Simmel, and G. A. Milton (Eds.), Early Experiences
and the Processes of Socialization. 1970

Richard Christie and Florence Geis, Studies in Machiavellianism. 1970

Paul G. Swingle (Ed.), The Structure of Conflict. 1970

Alvin Zander, Motives and Goals in Groups. 1971

Stanley Schachter, Emotion, Obesity, and Crime. 1971

Charles A. Kiesler, The Psychology of Commitment:
Experiments Linking Behavior to Belief. 1971

Jacobo A. Varela, Psychological Solutions to Social Problems:
An Introduction to Social Technology. 1971

David C. Glass and Jerome E. Singer, Urban Stress:
Experiments on Noise and Social Stressors. 1972

Ivan D. Steiner, Group Process and Productivity. 1972

Shelley Duval and Robert A. Wicklund, A Theory of Objective Self Awareness. 1972

Alice Ross Gold, Richard Christie, and Lucy Norman Friedman, Fists and Flowers:
A Social Psychological Interpretation of Student Dissent. 1976

Fists and Flowers

A Social Psychological
Interpretation of Student Dissent

Alice Ross Gold
Wesleyan University

Richard Christie
Columbia University

Lucy Norman Friedman
Columbia University

ACADEMIC PRESS   New York San Francisco London   1976
A Subsidiary of Harcourt Brace Jovanovich, Publishers

ACADEMIC PRESS, INC.
111 Fifth Avenue, New York, New York 10003

United Kingdom Edition published by
ACADEMIC PRESS, INC. (LONDON) LTD.
24/28 Oval Road, London NW1

Library of Congress Cataloging in Publication Data

Gold, Alice Ross.
    Fists and flowers.

    (Social psychology series)
    Bibliography: p.
    1.   Student movements.   I.   Christie, Richard,
joint author.   II.   Friedman, Lucy N., joint author.
III.   Title.
LA186.G59   378.1'98'1   75-19640
ISBN 0–12–287650–4

Contents

4 Ideology and Behavior: The Protester's Profile

5 Family Background and Protest Ideology

6 Academic and Demographic Variables Relating to Protest Ideology

7 The Social Context

Preface

In the spring of 1968 our offices and laboratories in the Social Psychology Department at Columbia University were occupied by student demonstrators. The events that followed generated for us a personal sense of excitement and political involvement, but they also sparked our curiosity as social psychologists. This book is an account of the research that grew out of these experiences.

Initially we were interested in the ideology of student dissidents and the process of radicalization. To what extent did student dissidents have a consistent pattern of beliefs? Were students' political attitudes becoming more radical? If so, how stable would the changes be? Were some students changing more than others? How would one describe the process of radicalization? In order to explore these questions, we created an attitude scale (the New Left scale), which we hoped would tap the prevailing ideology of the demonstrators. The scale was administered to a variety of samples, including high school students, college students, college dropouts (counterculture), policemen, and construction workers. In doing so we developed what we call the "protester's profile," a description of the ideology of the New Left using five subscales derived from a factor analysis of a larger pool of items. Three of the subscales are updated versions of Machiavellian and authoritarianism scales; two represent new ideological viewpoints.

The focus of the book is on these political attitudes. Using a panel sample of Columbia College students, we discuss the process of radicalization and the characteristics that differentiate those who became radicalized from those who did not. We also use data from college and noncollege samples to describe the relationship of attitudes to demographic, contextual, and academic variables. Our failure to replicate previously reported relationships suggests a change in the constituency of the New Left from the mid to the late 1960s. In addition, a major theme that emerges from all the analyses is youth's involvement with and orientation toward their peers versus their parents. We suspect that this orientation contributes significantly to the generation gap.

This book is a lesson in history, a social psychological analysis of an historical era. We also believe it adds to a general understanding of social movements and hope it will stimulate more research on the applicability of social psychological concepts to field settings.

Acknowledgments

The research on which this book is based would not have been possible without a gift to the Social Psychology Department at Columbia University from Joseph Klingenstein. In addition, two of the authors were supported by NIMH and NDEA Title VII training grants during the course of the research.

We are especially grateful to the late William W. Cummings who generously gave two class hours to us—one for filling out the questionnaires that stirred our curiosity and the other for a discussion of the findings. Dr. Cummings administered some attitude scales and made important observations about the Columbia crisis, which made us examine certain relationships critical to the direction of the research.

Many other people have contributed to the material in the following pages. Camilla Auger and Raymond Maurice encouraged us to develop and distribute the first questionnaire and commiserated with us as they also analyzed data generated from the 1968 crisis. Peter Waring as well as other members of radical groups provided useful insights into the New Left and helped us develop items for the attitude scale. Ned Anschuetz, Vincent Bozzone, Stanley Budner, David Carter, Abraham Chaplan, Judi Friedman, Edward J. Hyman, Theodore Norman, William Tracy, Joan Welkowitz, Daniel Yankelovich, Arthur York, and Richard Zweigenhaft administered our scale or modifications of it so that we could have data from diverse populations. We are grateful to all of them.

Kenneth King and the staff of the Columbia University Computer Center made their facilities available to us; Dean Stewart provided us with comparative data on the Columbia class of 1972; Jane Coleman ingeniously and carefully carried out the experiment on antiscientism; Mark Fridovich conducted personal interviews sensitively; Max Morales, Jim Pleasance, and Gail Christie assisted with data analysis. To them go our warm appreciation. We are also indebted to the many secretaries over the years who have typed and retyped the scales and earlier drafts of this manuscript.

Most of all, we wish to thank our respondents, especially those in the panel sample, for their patience and cooperation. It is they who provided the data that inspired this research.

A.R.G.
R.C.
L.N.F.[1]

---

[1] Currently at Vera Institute of Justice, New York, New York.

1
Introduction

The title of this book arose from thoughts about the apparent contradictions in the behavior of Vietnam War protesters, as reflected in two of the symbols of the late 1960s—the daisy of peace and innocence, and the red clenched fist of revolution that was stenciled on many walls. This juxtaposition of love of mankind with violent rebellion puzzled and intrigued us. This book is an account of how we attempted to interpret it.

Our focus is on the ideology of protesters during the late 1960s and how it related to behavior. We make no attempt at depth psychological interpretations, nor do we view participants in the protests of the 1960s as part of a recurring sociological pattern of youthful dissent. We are interested in the antecedents, correlates, and consequences of protest within a social psychological framework. Consequently, we have tried to remain close to the data, confining speculation to the minimum that is necessary for their interpretation. In addition, two broad implications of our research should be noted. First by focusing on the process of radicalization during a period of social upheaval, rather than retrospective to it, we hope to cast new and different light on an issue that has long interested historians and political theorists—who becomes radicalized and under what conditions. Second, for better or worse, many of the current generation of young adults were disenchanted with the institutions of American society in the late 1960s and early 1970s, and many of their experiences during those years had a significant, if not profound, effect on their development as individuals. As they now assume adult roles in society, it is important to try to understand more clearly the nature of their concern. We hope this book will help to further such an understanding.

Routes to Collaboration

The three of us came to this collaboration via different routes. The initial common denominators were association with the Department of Social Psychology[1] at Columbia University in the spring of 1968; a common interest in social psychology theory and research; and some familiarity with and, more importantly, curiosity about, the nature of student unrest. The dramatic events of April and May 1968, when students occupied (or "liberated") some of the buildings at Columbia and were removed (or "busted") by the police, and the consequent cessation of most academic activity (or "strike") for the remainder of the semester led to our comparing notes and reactions and thus to our working together.

We trust that whatever biases we may have had at the start have been modified by discussions of differences in interpretation and by an examination of the data. This is neither a committee report representing the blandest of consensus nor a coalition of two in a triad versus an unwritten minority report. Each of us has had an equal voice in the statements that appear in the subsequent chapters. In some cases one of us may have had a more equal voice than the others, but the messages conveyed by the data came through so strongly that they obscured minor differences in interpretation.

We have decided to split voices, for the first and last time in the book, and give individual accounts of the events of that late spring of 1968 at Columbia which laid the groundwork for our cooperation. The reader is referred to Grant (1969) or Kunen (1968) for a more complete description of the Columbia crisis itself.

STATEMENT BY RICHARD CHRISTIE

My interest in student protest can possibly be interpreted as a reaction formation against the ideological paucity of my formative years in small towns ranging geographically from Saskatchewan, where I was born, to others in Missouri, Kansas, Arkansas, and Oklahoma. The first Catholics I knew well enough to talk with were some fellow students, who were of predominantly Bohemian background, in a small town in western Oklahoma when a senior in high school. I never knew any Jews or blacks until after I had graduated from college and entered the Air Force. The same was even more true of self-proclaimed ex-Communists, alleged Communists, and other leftists.

As a graduate student in Berkeley after World War II, I was fascinated with the work then being done on *The Authoritarian Personality* (Adorno, Frenkel-Brunswik, Levinson, & Sanford, 1950). Their description, by means of personality and attitude measures, depicted with uncanny accuracy many of the

---

[1] Now part of the Psychology Department, Faculty of Pure Science.

people I had known in the heartland of America and in the Air Force. It seemed possible to investigate individuals of different ideological colorations by psychological techniques, a notion that was a revelation to me at the time.

The other major influences at Berkeley came from S. M. Lipset. We were working together on a survey in Oakland and in the course of our association I listened with rapt fascination to his accounts of pre-World War II leftist politics at the City College of New York and the political infighting among Stalinists, Trotskyites, Lovestoneites, and other splinter groups. The onset of the Cold War and the quiet generation of college students in the 1950s effectively made samples of leftists scarce or not easily obtainable, so the only work of mine that was remotely related to political activity was restricted to methodological critiques of Eysenck's palpably false equation of the personality of Communists and Fascists (Christie, 1956a,b).

In the mid-1950s, my major research concern became the behavior of those who were successful in manipulating others (Christie, 1970c). These Machiavellian-oriented individuals were not, it appeared, particularly ideological. There were, however, an abundance of them among the student body at Columbia, and for over the decade most of my free research time was devoted to experimental and field studies designed to determine under what circumstances persons with a manipulative bent were effective in exploiting their more trusting peers. The research had been largely completed by the spring of 1968, and my research interests were shifting toward laboratory studies of personality and situational variables relating to the evaluations persons made of others in face-to-face situations. These plans were temporarily shelved by the events of April and May 1968 at Columbia.

It seems incredible, in retrospect, that those events should have been so unexpected. In February of 1968 I had visited Howard University in Washington, D.C., and I remember my sense of surprise that students had actually occupied the dean's office during working hours on the day preceding my visit. [During the most famous sit-in previous to this—that of Sproul Hall at Berkeley on December 2-3, 1964—students had occupied the halls, but not the offices (Lipset & Wolin, 1965, pp. 163-164).] I had previously observed several teach-ins on the Vietnamese War at Columbia, the peace parade in May 1967, the march on the Pentagon of the previous November, and other antiwar rallies. None of these activities appeared particularly radical; they struck me more as a temporary catharsis for feelings of frustration at being unable to affect actions of the government that were felt to violate traditional American standards of justice and morality.

Only a few months later, Mathematics Hall at Columbia, which housed the offices of the Department of Social Psychology, was occupied. During the occupation some of our students were permitted entrance to the building to continue running experiments, so it was possible to obtain progress reports on events in the building. After the police had cleared the building, I inspected our quarters to determine what damage had been done (see Grant, 1969, pp. 185-187).

Contrary to published reports, the student dissidents occupying our quarters were well disciplined, kept the place neat, and did not engage in malicious destructive activity. Some questions about newspaper accounts were also raised by the fact that the issue of the *New York Times* of April 30, 1968, which appeared on the corner of Broadway and 116th Street at 6 A.M. (and had gone to press 2 hours before) carried a story of the night's activities based upon the original police time schedule. According to the *Times* account, Mathematics Hall had been cleared by 4 A.M.; in fact, it was not until about 4:45 A.M. that I had watched the last occupants being marched out of the building.

In addition to questions about these and other discrepancies between personal observations of events and published accounts of them, there was also the problem of trying to reconcile my impressions of student protesters with the instant analyses of their motivations offered by many "experts" who knew even less about the matter than I did. Given a personal history of an interest in political ideology and behavior and a professional history of over a score of years of research on individual predispositions and their interaction with situational variables, my subsequent behavior was highly predictable. When interested and curious, do research. And, given well-ingrained patterns of conceptualization and procedure (sometimes known as rigidity when observed in other people), it seemed natural to use as a springboard two areas of research with which I had some familiarity—authoritarianism and Machiavellianism.

STATEMENT BY LUCY NORMAN FRIEDMAN AND ALICE ROSS GOLD

In contrast to the more than two decades of evolution that resulted in Christie's interest in student activism, we became almost spontaneously involved. In the spring of 1968, as first-year graduate students at Columbia, our research interests were not yet defined. We were taking courses and helping to design and conduct experiments in social psychology when our schedules were disrupted by the crisis. Together with most students, we supported the student strike—we stopped research and started attending "liberation classes." Instead of studying carefully specified responses in a laboratory, we discussed the social behavior of students, faculty, and administration at a university in crisis.

It was difficult for any member of the Columbia community to feel detached about the events of that spring. The polarization within the student body and faculty, the extended news coverage, the interest, questions, and opinions of many outsiders all conveyed a sense of the import of the crisis to everyone concerned. We were not exceptions. Although we each felt strongly about some of the issues, neither of us had taken an active stand. We both were ambivalent about what our role should be. Perhaps our training had been such that before committing ourselves to action, we wanted to understand the scientific data. Of course, we also had personal reasons for not participating. (One of us, for example, was 8½ months pregnant.) Thus, for reasons not completely clear to each of us at the time, we merely observed the <u>liberation</u> of buildings, but at the same time continuously searched for information and understanding of the confusing events. [*handwritten margin note: NO QUOTES? OH BROTHER.*]

Our own conflicts over our roles in the demonstrations were heightened during a "liberation seminar" on the lawn one spring afternoon shortly after the police had cleared academic buildings of student protesters. No one in the class could ignore the irony that as graduate students in social psychology we were engaged in learning to analyze and understand human behavior, yet none of us was seizing the opportunity to study the significant social events occurring around us. A fellow student who had been in one of the communes in the liberated buildings reiterated this point. In the ensuing discussion we began to have regrets: *If only* we had been able to predict the communes, the "bust," and the strike, we then could have collected interesting data relevant to group dynamics, attitude changes, and crowd behavior, among many other topics. By the end of the class, several suggestions for still feasible field studies relating to the crisis were proposed. This was not an unusual conclusion for seminars; however what followed was. The two of us decided to take seriously some of the ideas that had been bandied about casually. Studying the crisis offered the compromise we sought. We would be involved professionally, but for the moment would not be committed to personal action.

Although the impact of the Columbia crisis was intense, with hindsight we recognize that our decision to study some aspect of it was more than a way of coping with the ambivalence we both felt at the time. The seemingly spontaneous decision of that May afternoon became the genesis of research because it enabled us to gain some firsthand experience with socially relevant issues and field methods, two areas that we had both come to Columbia interested in but had found sorely lacking in our education up to that point.

The focus of our research idea, however, did not spring from vacuums in our education. Rather it was the opposite; for the past year we had been intensively studying attitudes, mostly within the context of consistency theories. Our familiarity with these theories, which deal with an inconsistency between attitudes and actions, led us to consider the Columbia crisis in terms of relationship between the behavior and beliefs of the students involved. Although we had no systematic data—only our own reactions and observations—the "bust" seemed to us a natural experiment that could very easily be interpreted as supporting consistency theory. Before it had occurred, most students were only mildly sympathetic to the demonstrators; yet involvement in confrontation with the police, although vicarious for most, appeared to have led to a dramatic polarization of attitudes.

We did realize, of course, that we were too late to test such a hypothesis, having no precrisis measure of attitudes. Thus, we decided on a panel design that would investigate the long-term effects of the crisis. In this way we would make maximum use of the field situation, which seemed more receptive to longitudinal studies than did the laboratory. We also felt that a comprehensive study of a social issue (i.e., the process of change as a function of political participation) necessitated the periodic retesting of subjects. Most real-life changes, we argued, do not happen within a few minutes (as often appears the case from laboratory research) but, instead, occur over a period of time.

In sum, the decision to begin the research, although initially sparked by the liberation class, reflected both an interest in the relationship of attitudes to behavior, stemming from our extensive exposure to consistency theories, and an interest in dealing with social problems in natural settings, stemming from a lack of exposure to them.

Before embarking on the research, we investigated other projects that had sprung up as a result of the Columbia crisis. Finding none of them directly relevant to our interests, we designed our own questionnaire, which focused on (1) participation in specific activities during the demonstrations, (2) attitudes toward the student demands and toward the actions of participants before and after the police "bust," (3) knowledge of what had happened, and (4) beliefs in possible long- and short-term outcomes of the crisis.

In retrospect we realize our research design was too ambitious. We envisioned two separate panel studies, the first involving those individuals, both pro- and antistrike, who had participated in some way in the crisis (from signing petitions to occupying buildings) and the second involving the incoming freshman class at Columbia, the class of 1972. We expected to continue both of these studies for 3 or 4 years.

The immediate problem confronting us was how to gather subjects for the first panel. After spending several days searching for someone to help us reach the most radical students, we finally found an SDS (Students for a Democratic Society) leader who agreed to let us pass out the questionnaires to those attending a meeting for persons who had been arrested during the police bust. However, as fate would have it, the questionnaires never left our hands. Approximately half an hour before the scheduled time of the meeting, Hamilton Hall, the main classroom building for the college, was occupied by striking students once again. The campus was totally disrupted, and the meeting was canceled.

Because of this inopportune turn of events, we were about to abandon the entire project when, quite by chance, two graduate students in sociology, who had heard of our research, asked us to work with them. Together we devised a new, more sophisticated questionnaire, which was mailed to a large number of Columbia students who had been involved on both sides of the demonstrations.

As the summer wore on, we began to think seriously about our research aims, which up to this point had been amorphous. It became more and more apparent to us that, if we intended to focus on the process of radicalization, our primary concern should be the planned panel study of the entering freshmen. As opposed to the crisis study, it offered us the possibility of a controlled design—a homogeneous sample, assurance that most members would be at Columbia for 4 years, and the opportunity to obtain adequate pretest information—which would enable us to gather more definitive data on the topic. We could measure attitudes upon arrival at Columbia and wait to see the effects of confrontation and demonstration. Because of the state of flux of the university and the impact of the 1968 Democratic Convention, we firmly (although mistakenly) believed another disruption would occur at Columbia during the students' first year there. As the advantages of a freshman panel study became obvious, we increasingly devoted our energies to it, at the expense of the panel study of crisis participants.

Whence We Proceeded

Programs of research are usually marked by continuity, new studies being based upon reconciling discrepancies found in previous experiments. This leads to the well-known process of finding out more and more about less and less, and thus creating an ever-tightening spiral that is usually broken only by something sufficiently dramatic to question the premises underlying the whole enterprise.

In our case, the "something sufficiently dramatic" occurred (i.e., the Columbia demonstrations in 1968), but instead of forcing us to reexamine what we had been doing, it spurred us to embark on a totally new avenue of research, one much broader than those with which we had dealt before. Despite both the novelty of the event and our differences in formal research and informal experiences, we all responded to the crisis as an event that could be conceptualized in terms of familiar social psychological relationships between changes in attitudes and in behavior. Although over the past 20 years the study of these relationships by psychologists had become increasingly involved with the pursuit of abstract principles underlying human interaction, we felt these theories and methodologies could aptly be applied to the real-life problems of social and political change.

We then began, as is usual with new research programs, to examine the existing literature and data on student dissent. Whereas most earlier studies did not deal with the particular question of politicization, which was our original concern, we did find some materials that helped us further define our research interests. Studies done early in the protest movement, such as those by Flacks (1967) and by Westby and Braungart (1966), gave evidence that radical students were likely to come from socially advantaged families and that these students were comparatively more likely to have high test scores, have attended elite schools, and have made good grades. Their parents were better educated and tended to be urban, Jewish, and to have a history of involvement in radical political activity in the 1930s. Although we accepted these findings when we started collecting data, there are serious questions as to whether they can be generalized to the samples tested since 1968, at least in the schools for which we have material.

Another provocative source was Zweigenhaft's research with Columbia College students (see Appendix A). His purpose was to compare evaluations of pictures of bearded and nonbearded hypothetical college draft evaders in order to explore a possible link between looking off-beat and behaving in a socially deviant way (resisting the draft). What triggered our interest was that ratings on a bipolar checklist indicated that Columbia freshmen and seniors evaluated hypothetical draft resisters (shorn or unshorn) more favorably on 12 of 14 personality dimensions than they did a hypothetical student who enlisted in the army. Since these data were collected in the spring of 1968 prior to the excitement at Columbia, they pointed to a positive radical sentiment which probably provided the foundation for the demonstrations a couple of months later.

Immediately after the crisis during the spring of 1968, our research direction was critically influenced by data that had been collected in the introductory psychology class at Columbia College in the fall of 1967, approximately 6 months before the occupation of buildings. These data consisted of responses to several short Likert-type scales. William W. Cumming, who taught the introductory psychology course, observed that during the period of occupation, some of his fall-term students were to be seen peering out through the windows of Grayson Kirk's presidential office or perched on the ledge outside the windows, while others of the class were marching outside in counterprotest. When the list of those arrested in the first police bust became available, his casual comment aroused our curiosity. Checking the list of arrestees against that of the students who had been enrolled in the course in the fall indicated that 26 of the 145 who had completed the scale responses were among the 524 Columbia students arrested in the bust. The scale data were then examined to find out whether or not arrestees and nonarrestees differed in their range of scores. One highly significant difference was found. On a scale called Traditional Moralism, which measures acceptance of conventional values, arrestees were much more likely to have a low score than those members of the class who, for one reason or another, did not have their names on police blotters. This could easily have been predicted upon the basis of research on the California F-scale (authoritarianism). What was of particular relevance, however, was that this difference was accounted for by the one-sixth of the students who had the highest scores, none of whom had been arrested. For the other 119 students, it was impossible to predict on the basis of their scale scores who was and who was not likely to have been arrested for dissident behavior. This suggested that the scales, based upon over a quarter of a century of research on college and other samples, were *not* tapping a range of predispositions toward involvement in campus protest, but only refusal to get involved in the protest activities. In other words, it appeared that there were new ideological currents among the students in 1968 that were not being captured in the items used.

There was further cause for reflection about the failure of existing items to capture the disenchantment of the majority of the students tested. In response to open-ended questions about political ideology from crisis participants, many students put forward ideas that had not appeared in earlier attitude scales, even those developed in the mid-1960s. One point should be particularly emphasized. However elegantly or inelegantly responses were phrased, a persistently recurring theme was the pervasive distrust of the institutions and legitimate channels of change in contemporary society.

Some Words about Methods and Organization

Given our common interests, how best to proceed? Our first concern was the construction of relevant measures and standardized scales for purposes of comparing groups and measuring attitudinal changes over time. Once we were satisfied that it was possible to devise such measures, we began to formulate research questions. To what extent did student dissidents have a consistent ideology? What were the characteristics of those whom we could identify as protest prone? Under what conditions were such dissident proclivities enhanced or modified?

For reasons of both availability (students at one's own university) and relevance (Columbia at the time had a high proportion of student rebels), we decided to focus on students at Columbia College, the well-known undergraduate, liberal arts school at the University. The incoming class of 1972 was selected as the best target. Material on other groups is used to illustrate and support particular findings, especially because some of our results from this sample run counter to currently popular beliefs about student activists. For example, we found no relationship between level of parental education and student radicalism among members of the class of 1972. This was contrary to published reports on students in general. However, since the educational level of Columbia parents is not only extremely high but also not distributed normally, we collected data on a high school sample where there was a much more typical distribution of parental education. Data from other samples were made available to us by colleagues who, because of their interest in the research, had administered the scales themselves.

There are limiting factors in interpreting the data. Since this research was not funded by a grant, our financial resources were frugally expended. This meant that it was not feasible to sally forth to the most relevant sample, wherever it might be, to collect information. In actual practice, however, this was not a major restriction. As noted before, our interest is not in estimating percentages of dissident students for a particular kind of college or university, but in the understanding of radicalism. In fact, utilizing an informal network of communication among colleagues and other friends has enabled us to collect material from diverse samples.

Another obvious problem concerns the cooperation, not only of those who have helped us collect data in various samples, but among respondents as well. It is difficult to make an overall appraisal. Some committed radicals have refused to cooperate on the grounds that even if we were not working for the FBI, the results would be used by college administrators to screen out potential trouble-makers. Equally committed conservatives have refused because the investigation was "obviously Communist-inspired." On the other hand, some dedicated revolutionists have been very helpful in recruiting respondents, as have been some conservatives. However, during the course of the study, we noticed an increasing concern among students about the potential misuse of the data collected. It has resulted in a reluctance—and an occasional refusal—to complete the scales. This problem is discussed in greater detail later in the book.

The book is divided into three sections. Chapters 2 and 3 deal with the basic methodological tools and procedures. Summary tables of the samples discussed in the remainder of the book are provided in Chapter 3, in order that readers uninterested in the details of the sampling methods can get an overview of the range of the data without wading through the technical aspects that researchers feel committed to discuss for the benefit of their academic peers and posterity.

The second section contains four chapters, which examine the correlates of radicalism, that is, the characteristics distinguishing individuals endorsing New Left beliefs from those who do not. In this section we examine common stereotypes of radicals and analyze their veridicality with respect to the individuals from whom we gathered data.

In the last section, comprising Chapters 8 and 9, the process of radicalization is explored in detail. Although the material for these chapters is based entirely on data collected from a panel sample of Columbia College class of 1972 students, the reader will find the themes that emerge strikingly similar to those of earlier chapters. Chapter 10, the concluding chapter, summarizes the findings and implications of the research.

2

The Development
of Scales Relevant to
New Left Ideology

At the time that we became interested in research on the New Left, there was no apparent agreement as to whether or not student dissidents had a coherent ideology. Our first task, therefore, was an exploration and analysis of expressions of opinion by students to see if there was in fact any measurable set of values that differentiated politically active students from others. Our search for such a set of values and a description of the measures we finally developed for them are discussed in this chapter. These measures or variants of them form the nucleus of all the subsequent chapters.

On the Measurement of Relevant Values

Since most of our comparisons use scores on attitude scales as dependent variables, it is crucial for an understanding of what follows to know what the scores on these scales mean. This is especially important since three of the scales are greatly modified versions of older scales and two of the scales are completely new.

Unfortunately, we could not rely exclusively on existing scales because they did not capture much of the content of the rhetoric on the Columbia campus in the spring of 1968. This does not mean, of course, that all ideas current on the campus that hectic spring were novel. It rather indicates that they had not previously been expressed by a socially conspicuous group in such a way as to spur someone to attempt to capture them in questionnaires.

It was noted in the introduction that some attitude scores were available on members of the introductory psychology class who had been arrested during the police bust at Columbia in the spring of 1968. These students had taken four 7-item scales, dubbed the FacMac scales. These scales were based upon a factor analysis of responses to 50 items by a national sample of college students in 1964 (Christie & Lehmann, 1970). The 50 items came from old scales measuring Machiavellianism, authoritarianism, and anomia. Each of the four scales was composed of the 7 Likert-format items loading highest on four factors emerging from the factor analysis. The first scale or factor was labeled "Duplicity," and most of the items came from the Machiavellianism scale and refer to the importance of honesty and candor (or the lack of them) in interpersonal relations. The second factor was interpreted as reflecting a combination of agreement response set and a negative view of society in general; it was dubbed "Affirmative (because of the presumed effect of agreement response set) Negativism" (because of the sour world view). The third factor was titled "Distrust in People," and a high score was made by rejecting reverse Machiavellian and Anomia statements about the goodness of man. The fourth scale represented an acceptance of F-scale or authoritarian items; this factor was labeled "Traditional Moralism." We decided to include these 28 items in the exploratory pool for the present study in order to provide an established frame of reference, which would make the interpretation of new items clearer.

A number of new items were then designed to cover a broad spectrum of student opinion relating to what we, at the time, perceived to be relevant issues of the New Left and its opposition. We found no dearth of possible statements, using notes and recollections of what was said (loudly if not always clearly) at public meetings, statements appearing in flyers and underground newspapers, and responses to open-ended questions on the part of participants in the spring disruptions. In addition to these sources, we utilized ideas expressed in earlier attitude scales, but couched them in comtemporary political language. However, we did impose two restrictions on our statements because we were more interested in underlying values than in reactions to specific events:

1. To give the scale generality in time, we eliminated all items referring to the Vietnam War because we (naively) thought that these items would only have a transitory relevance. Correspondingly, all items that dealt with university reform and curricula were discounted because we did not want to limit the use of the scales to college samples.

2. No questions on the specific tactics endorsed by various dissident groups, such as the Weathermen or the Afro-American Society, were included. Again, the rationale was a greater interest in basic values than in the type of tactics adopted by various groups (and subgroups), which changed quickly with events.

Among the hundreds of statements we designed, there was some degree of redundancy. In an attempt to impose organization, we examined and classified the items. We divided the content into four categories: world view, goals, tactics, and life styles. We felt that these categories reflected the four most important facets of the New Left ideology. The life-style items tended to be inspired by counter-culture ideas emanating from politically oriented groups. The world-view items represented general statements about the structure of society. To give the scale breadth, we sought for each category items that would be agreed or disagreed upon by members of four student groups ranging from the radical Students for a Democratic Society (SDS) to the conservative Young Americans for Freedom (YAF). Eventually, we phased out the two moderate groups because we felt that if an item was endorsed by "liberals" but rejected by radicals and conservatives, we would have difficulty interpreting scale scores. For this reason we used the eight-cell format shown in Table 2.1.

Each statement in the existing pool was studied to see if it fit into one of the eight cells. We then devised new items to complete the sparsely filled cells and eliminated items from overpopulated cells in order to have a roughly equal number of items in each cell. Some student activists were also asked to evaluate the items in terms of how they thought various groups would respond to them, to suggest new items, and to suggest changes in existing ones that would bring them closer to the student vernacular.

In all, we developed 62 new items, which were coupled with the 28 items from the FacMac scales to form a 90-item scale. The items were randomly ordered in a questionnaire that was cast in a traditional Likert format with a range of seven options for response on each item: strongly disagree, somewhat disagree, slightly disagree, no opinion or neutral, slightly agree, somewhat agree, strongly agree. For the 62 new items, these options were scored from 1 to 7, with 7 the hypothesized New Left response.

Table 2.1
Categories of Questions That Formed the Basis of the New Left Scale

	Student groups	
Category	SDS (radical)	YAF (conservative)
World view		
Goals		
Tactics		
Life style		

This 90-item questionnaire, along with other materials, was administered to 153 members of the class of 1972 in November of 1968, less than 2 months after they had arrived at Columbia. The first analysis used a part-whole correlational technique to compare responses to each of the 90 items with the summed responses to the 62 new items. We found that 56 of the 62 items correlated significantly with this total score at a probability level of .05 or better, indicating that almost all these new items were being responded to along a New Left dimension. In addition, the 20 items with the highest part-whole correlations were new items; none were from the FacMac scales (see Appendix B-1). This high degree of internal consistency suggested that we were dealing with an attitudinal domain that had at least a fair degree of coherence.

We next examined the intercorrelations among the five subscales on the 90-item questionnaire (i.e., the four FacMac scales and the New Left ideology items). Traditional Moralism, Distrust, and Affirmative Negativism all correlated significantly with New Left ideology (see Table 2.2). The highest correlation between New Left ideology and the FacMac scales was with Traditional Moralism; this finding parallels the results of the arrestee-nonarrestee data from the spring of 1968. Similarly, the discrepancy score between Distrust and Duplicity, which we had found to be marginally related to behavior during the 1968 Columbia demonstrations, correlated significantly with the summed scores on

Table 2.2
Interscale Correlations of FacMac Scales and Original New Left Ideology Measure

	New Left Ideology	Affirmative Negativism	Duplicity	Distrust in People	Traditional Moralism	Distrust minus Duplicity
New Left Ideology (62-item scale)	—	$.19^a$	−.13	$.33^a$	$-.42^a$	$.34^a$
Affirmative Negativism		—	$.35^a$	$.32^a$	−.15	−.07
Duplicity			—	.14	−.12	$-.73^a$
Distrust in People				—	$-.23^a$	$.58^a$
Traditional Moralism					—	−.06
Distrust minus Duplicity						—

$^a p<.05$ two-tailed. (All probabilities reported in the book are based on two-tailed tests of significance.)

the New Left ideology items. A pattern emerges from these data that reverses earlier findings in the Machiavellian literature. Unlike previous research, in which Distrust and Duplicity were correlated with other attitude scales in the same direction—either both negatively or both positively—here they related in opposite directions to New Left ideology. Duplicity was negatively correlated and Distrust was positively correlated. This was not true of the relationship of these two scales to Affirmative Negativism or to Traditional Moralism. The significance of these results will be discussed later in the chapter.

A Factor Analysis of Responses to Attitude Items

The degree of internal consistency along the New Left continuum was gratifying. More items discriminated among high and low scorers than was true of either the work on the *F*-scale reported in *The Authoritarian Personality* (Adorno *et al.,* 1950) or that on the Mach scale in *Studies in Machiavellianism* (Christie, 1970b). Because previous experience suggested that more than one dimension might be involved, even among the new items, a factor analysis of the responses to the 90 items was performed. The 90 × 90 matrix of item intercorrelations was subjected to a principal components factor analysis with varimax rotations. It was easiest to interpret a five-factor solution of the relationships among the items. The 12 items with the highest loading on each of the factors were retained and formed five individual scales. (Items not retained are in Appendix B-1.) These scales form the basic dependent measures of the research.

There are several points that should be noted. Some of the items have loadings on more than one factor; in such cases the item is assigned to the factor on which it has the highest loading. Second, in the descriptions of each factor, which follow, interpretation of the meaning of each factor is most influenced by the items with the highest loadings on it. (The tables are presented with the items listed according to their factor loadings.) The interpretations are also affected by the presence or absence of items loading on similar factors in previous research. Finally, it must be borne in mind that labeling of a factor is a highly subjective art. Our interpretations are colored by the objective loadings of the items on the factors as well as by our facility, or lack of it, to capture in a brief phrase what seems to be the underlying theme in a particular scale. For example, we labeled one scale, "New Left Philosophy"; others might have labeled it "Sophomoric Soft-headedness," "Neo-Rousseauism," "Romantic Idealism," or "anti-Agnewism." In understanding the scores to be reported on different samples in the following pages, the reader would be well advised to scan the items in each scale and interpret them for him or herself, so that the particular idiosyncratic label chosen by us does not impose artificial restrictions on his interpretation of the scale.

TRADITIONAL MORALISM

We view the Traditional Moralism scale as a conceptual descendant of the original California F-scale, which used endorsement of an interrelated set of middle-America conventional values to measure right-wing authoritarian proclivities. The particular items in the present version are the result of experience gained (1) in using the original form and finding marked differences in a variety of geographical sections of the country in both mean item acceptance and relationships among items (Christie & Garcia, 1951), (2) in reanalysis of the original and subsequent research on the F-scale (Christie, 1954; Christie & Cook, 1958), (3) in examining the old items and constructing new ones to alleviate the response set problem (Christie, Havel, & Seidenberg, 1958), and (4) in factor analyzing the revised scale on a national sample of 1782 college students (Christie & Lehmann, 1970).

Regarding previous research, two important points need to be mentioned. In hundreds of studies using the original F-scale and its variants, certain relationships between scores on the scale and demographic variables have appeared. For example, high scorers are more likely to be older, less educated, politically conservative, and less sophisticated than low scorers. In addition, the internal structure of the scale has been shown to be diffuse. The authors of *The Authoritarian Personality* posited nine underlying psychological dimensions, but neither these nor any other specific ones have been empirically verified in the original research or in at least a dozen subsequent factor analyses with which we are familiar. This lack of psychometric purity does not necessarily indicate that the basic concept of the scale is untenable; rather, it appears to be caused by the great variability of responses to particular items resulting from differing interpretations of them as they are cast in the light of constantly changing social conditions. We believe that our scale, because of its contemporaneity, taps fairly accurately the fundamental notions of the original F-scale from the standpoint of the 1968 scene.

The 12 items on the Traditional Moralism factor are listed in Table 2.3. Of the 12 items, 8 were developed by us in this study, including the 3 with the highest loadings, which emphasize law and order and the virtues of hard work. All 4 of the remaining items are from previous versions of the F-scale. (See Appendix B-1 for complete listing of origin of items.)

MACHIAVELLIAN TACTICS

Twenty years ago, items designed to tap proclivities toward interpersonal manipulation were developed from statements in Machiavelli's *The Prince* and

Table 2.3
Factor I: Traditional Moralism

Item	Factor loading				
	I	II	III	IV	V
Police should not hesitate to use force to maintain order.	+.693	+.251	−.123	−.128	+.029
The right to private property is sacred.	+.617	+.397	+.034	−.040	−.254
If people worked hard at their jobs, they would reap the full benefits of our society.	+.583	+.215	−.284	+.010	−.120
Most people who get ahead in the world lead clean, moral lives.	+.556	−.085	−.264	+.053	−.010
Every person should have complete faith in a supernatural power whose decisions he obeys without question.	+.541	+.086	−.035	+.004	−.129
People ought to pay more attention to new ideas, even if they seem to go against the American way of life.	−.525	+.053	+.154	+.065	+.023
A problem with most older people is that they have learned to accept society as it is, not as it should be.	−.524	−.024	+.150	+.383	−.078
If it weren't for the rebellious ideas of youth, there would be less progress in the world.	−.521	−.172	−.050	+.296	−.012
The very existence of our long-standing social norms demonstrates their value.	+.498	+.306	−.237	−.074	−.033
The findings of science may someday show that many of our most cherished beliefs are wrong.	−.444	+.225	−.059	+.003	+.103
The solution for contemporary problems lies in striking at their roots, no matter how much destruction might occur.	−.413	+.099	−.008	+.340	+.371
Even though institutions have worked well in the past, they must be destroyed if they are not effective now.	−.412	−.064	−.022	+.310	+.281

The Discourses. As opposed to those from the *F*-scale, these items have not, by and large, correlated with most measures of social position or ideology (Christie, 1970a), although they are related to manipulative behavior in a wide variety of experimental situations (Geis & Christie, 1970). This relationship is true, however, only in situations in which (1) the participants are face-to-face, rather than interacting with simulated or nonpresent others, (2) there is latitude for improvisation (i.e., participants are free to deviate in their responses, rather than having fixed options), and (3) irrelevant affect is involved (e.g., when participants are dealing with emotional rather than neutral issues). It seems plausible that situations of political confrontation, where a myriad of possibilities for the use of guile or deceit can exist, fit these three conditions.

With the exception of two items written for the present research, all the items in Table 2.4 come from the Duplicity and Affirmative Negativism scales of the FacMac scale.

An inspection of the items indicates that they reflect a hard-boiled, pragmatic, and markedly nonidealistic view of the way in which one should deal with others.

Table 2.4
Factor II: Machiavellian Tactics

| | Factor loading | | | | |
Item	I	II	III	IV	V
The best way to handle people is to tell them what they want to hear.	+.085	+.585	−.009	−.003	−.012
It is wise to flatter important people.	+.004	+.528	−.075	−.198	−.069
Next to health, money is the most important thing in life.	+.112	+.494	+.011	−.048	−.061
Anyone who completely trusts anyone else is asking for trouble.	+.073	+.477	+.232	−.017	−.198
Most of our social problems could be solved if we could somehow get rid of the immoral, crooked, and feebleminded people.	+.214	+.473	+.052	+.134	+.032
It is safest to assume that all people have a vicious streak and it will come out when they are given a chance.	−.067	+.446	+.063	−.066	−.041
All in all, it is better to be humble and honest than to be important and dishonest.	+.135	−.442	−.062	+.391	−.212
Voting must be a pragmatic rather than moral decision.	+.109	+.427	−.087	−.253	−.173
If you try hard enough, you can usually get what you want.	+.360	+.417	−.259	+.025	−.132
When you ask someone to do something for you, it is best to give the real reasons for wanting it rather than giving reasons which carry more weight.	+.182	−.396	+.087	+.266	+.027
Competition encourages excellence.	+.210	+.394	−.376	−.080	+.368
It is important that people be involved in the present, rather than concerned with the past or future.	−.092	+.388	+.092	+.360	−.062

MACHIAVELLIAN CYNICISM

Most of the items loading on this factor (see Table 2.5) come from two sources. Those with the highest factor loadings are from the Distrust in People scale of the FacMac scales. The last five items of the list are new; they reflect a pessimistic outlook about the viability of contemporary America. The major

Table 2.5
Factor III: Machiavellian Cynicism

Item	Factor loading				
	I	II	III	IV	V
Most people can still be depended on to come through in a pinch.	+.303	−.041	−.624	+.138	−.114
Most people in government are not really interested in the problems of the average man.	−.114	+.075	+.567	+.241	+.327
Most people will go out of their way to help someone else.	+.334	−.097	−.540	+.168	+.119
Being put in positions of leadership brings out the best in men.	+.104	+.291	−.522	+.036	−.053
Most people don't realize how much our lives are controlled by plots hatched in secret places.	−.053	+.143	+.475	+.148	+.226
You can never achieve freedom within the framework of contemporary American society.	−.358	−.090	+.458	+.311	+.332
Most people are basically good and kind.	+.210	−.256	−.437	+.281	+.061
It is possible to modify our institutions so that blacks can be incorporated on an equal basis in our contemporary society.	+.071	+.044	−.424	+.002	−.343
An individual can find his true identity only by detaching himself from formal ideologies.	−.060	−.031	+.423	+.188	−.197
Representative democracy can respond effectively to the needs of the people.	+.066	+.111	−.401	−.267	−.334
The bureaucracy of American society makes it impossible to live and work spontaneously.	−.277	−.087	+.386	+.199	+.155
Freedom of expression should be denied to racist and neofascistic movements.	+.293	+.040	+.354	+.012	+.204
Most men are brave.	+.274	−.113	−.304	+.308	+.150

theme of the scale, then, seems to be a lack of faith in the entire social system—both its structure and, more important, the individuals who work within it.

This factor has been dubbed Machiavellian Cynicism because the key items come from the Mach IV scale (Christie & Lehmann, 1970) and, unlike Machiavellian Tactics, it has philosophical rather than pragmatic connotations.

NEW LEFT PHILOSOPHY

An inspection of the items on this factor (see Table 2.6) indicates a common theme of disenchantment with current society and a belief, almost Rousseauean in nature, that man is inherently good, but that society has corrupted him.

Eleven of the 12 items are original to this research. The single exception ("no sane, normal decent person . . . ") comes from the old *F*-scale; in this context, it appears no longer related to a conventional viewpoint but, rather, to what seems to be a denial of baseness in human nature.

REVOLUTIONARY TACTICS

This scale is entirely composed of items that have not been used in previous research (see Table 2.7). The notions embodied in it reflect a view of contemporary social institutions as nonsalvageable and a belief in the necessity of violent social change. Since differences in scores on this scale will play a major part in the analyses that follow, scrutiny by the reader of the items on it is crucial for understanding the meaning of the shorthand term "Revolutionary Tactics" in the discussions that follow.

Some Comments about the Scales

Our initial four-part classification scheme used in constructing the scale is reflected in the factor analysis. Many of the items written for the "life-style" category have high loadings on the Traditional Moralism scale; those reflecting "world view" and "goals" fall on New Left Philosophy; and "tactics" items form a factor of their own—Revolutionary Tactics.

It is perhaps of greater significance that three of the factors identified on the FacMac scales are closely paralleled by the first three scales described here. Machiavellian Tactics is similar to the one called Duplicity, Machiavellian Cynicism is an amplified version of Distrust in People, and Traditional Moralism seems best to describe an equivalent factor in both studies. It seems, then, that these three concepts still are central to the attitudinal structure of college students.

New Left Philosophy is composed of items all scored so that agreement is high on the dimension. It, therefore, might be construed simply as an agreement

Table 2.6
Factor IV: New Left Philosophy

Item	Factor loading				
	I	II	III	IV	V
Real participatory democracy should be the basis for a new society.	−.179	−.190	+.091	+.572	−.154
Although men are intrinsically good, they have developed institutions which force them to act in opposition to this basic nature.	−.037	−.121	−.149	+.569	−.031
People should not do research which can be used in ways which are contrary to the social good.	+.005	−.244	+.152	+.491	+.040
If the structure of our society becomes nonrepressive, people will be happy.	−.104	−.100	+.007	+.486	+.002
A social scientist should not separate his political responsibilities from his professional role.	−.162	+.072	+.015	+.455	+.080
The United States needs a complete re-structuring of its basic institutions.	−.378	−.183	+.248	+.450	+.213
While man has great potential for good, society brings out primarily the worst in him.	−.089	+.138	+.252	+.447	+.167
The "Establishment" unfairly controls every aspect of our lives; we can never be free until we are rid of it.	−.408	−.138	+.409	+.440	+.306
No sane, normal, decent person could even think of hurting a close friend or relative.	+.222	+.108	+.138	+.436	+.070
The structure of our society is such that self-alienation is inevitable.	−.157	−.377	+.125	+.431	+.115
You learn more from 10 minutes in a po-litical protest than from 10 hours of re-search in a library.	−.117	+.018	+.022	+.430	+.183
Groups with a formal structure tend to stifle creativity among their members.	−.052	+.038	+.252	+.348	+.121

response set scale devoid of content. However, indiscriminate agreement usually occurs when the referents in an item are unclear or otherwise ambiguous to a respondent. The words and phrases used in the New Left Philosophy items were part of the common language at Columbia in 1968 (e.g., "participatory democracy," "the Establishment," "becomes nonrepressive"), and as such had consensual meaning to most of the students. It is highly probable, however, that agreement with many of these statements on the part of less sophisticated

Table 2.7
Factor V: Revolutionary Tactics

Item	Factor loading				
	I	II	III	IV	V
There are legitimate channels for reform which must be exhausted before attempting disruption.	+.236	+.162	−.038	−.170	−.635
We must strive for the democratization of decision-making bodies within the existing government.	−.157	+.162	+.027	+.180	−.614
Compromise is essential for progress.	+.063	+.213	−.148	−.024	−.590
Although our society has to be changed, violence is not a justified means.	+.402	+.008	−.023	+.016	−.587
Change is our society should be based primarily on popular elections.	+.252	+.033	−.153	+.301	−.559
Disruption is preferable to dialogue for changing our society.	−.175	+.044	+.219	+.258	+.527
Extensive reform in society only serves to perpetuate the evils; it will never solve problems.	+.300	−.027	+.177	+.169	+.517
The courts are a useful vehicle for responsible change.	.000	−.005	−.340	−.283	−.521
Anyone who breaks the law because he thinks it is wrong, should be willing to stand trial.	+.309	−.016	+.004	−.037	−.500
Authorities must be put in an intolerable position, so that they will be forced to respond with repression and thus show their illegitimacy.	−.295	+.012	+.140	+.363	+.478
Radicals of the left are as much a threat to the rights of the individual as are the radicals of the right.	+.199	+.260	−.113	−.320	−.447
A mass revolutionary party should be created.	−.424	−.133	+.112	+.276	+.448

respondents might occur because their referents were different from those of students on the politicized campus. If one does not know what "real participatory democracy" means in a radical context, the words have a positive flavor. (Who would be for an "illusionary, exclusive dictatorship"?). To Columbia respondents "the Establishment" referred to the military-industrial complex; to a Republican wheat farmer in Kansas it more likely referred to the Eastern Liberal Establishment. This possible response set may, of course, be one of the reasons why we subsequently found high scores on the New Left Philosophy scale among groups that we considered "moderate" and even "conservative."

Because some of the items we wrote were so closely tied to New Left phraseology (especially at Columbia in 1968), an attempt was made to remove much of the jargon so as to make the items more comprehensible to the average person. Many of the samples on whom data are reported took a revised form of the scales (see Appendix B-2). In retrospect, we think we erred. There are subtle, but major, differences between the two versions. In simplifying the language, some of the revised items lost their "barricade" flavor, and agreement with them probably represents a less radical viewpoint than agreement with the original items.

Relationships among the Scales

Table 2.8 contains the relevant information about factor scale intercorrelations, means, and reliabilities from the original sample of 153 Columbia freshmen. The reliabilities are high for 12-item scales, but it must be remembered that they were computed on the most discriminating items for this sample.

An examination of the intercorrelations among the scales indicates in most cases what would have been predicted, given the previously reported relationships of the total New Left scale with the FacMac scales (Table 2.2). The two new scales—New Left Philosophy and Revolutionary Tactics—are positively correlated with each other, although perhaps not as highly as one might have expected. Traditional Moralism is negatively related to New Left Philosophy and is even more negatively related to the extreme anti-Establishment items on Revolutionary Tactics. The nonsignificant correlation between Machiavellian Tactics and Machiavellian Cynicism, the positive correlations between Machiavellian Cynicism on the one hand and New Left Philosophy and Revolutionary Tactics on the other, and the negative correlations between Machiavellian Tactics and the two latter scales replicate the prior findings observed between the original measures of New Left ideology and the FacMac Duplicity and Distrust in People scales. In addition, the strength of these correlations does not appear to be spuriously caused by a few respondents. An inspection of the scatter plot of the correlation between Machiavellian Tactics and Machiavellian Cynicism, for example, reveals a substantial number of students with either high cynicism and low tactics scores or low cynicism and high tactics scores. As noted, such a relationship contradicts the results of a great deal of research done in the late 1950s and early 1960s on earlier generations of college students. At that time the two Machiavellian scales were invariably positively correlated, the magnitude of the correlations being around .40 or .50 (Christie, 1970b).

The positive relationship between Machiavellian Tactics and Traditional Moralism should be noted. With these same respondents the FacMac Duplicity scale correlated negatively, although not significantly so, with the FacMac version of

Table 2.8
Intercorrelations, Means, and Reliabilities of the Five Factor Scales ($N = 153$)

	Traditional Moralism	Machiavellian Tactics	Machiavellian Cynicism	New Left Philosophy	Revolutionary Tactics	Reliability
Traditional Moralism	—	.39[a]	-.26[a]	-.39[a]	-.52[a]	.85
Machiavellian Tactics	—	—	-.01	-.23[a]	-.35[a]	.73
Machiavellian Cynicism	—	—	—	.39[a]	.39[a]	.78
New Left Philosophy	—	—	—	—	.39[a]	.82
Revolutionary Tactics	—	—	—	—	—	.80
Item mean scores	2.85	3.44	3.84	3.75	2.69	
SD	1.12	1.01	1.04	1.09	1.11	

[a] $p < .05$.

Traditional Moralism (Table 2.2). Although Machiavellianism has not typically been found to be related to authoritarianism (Christie, 1970a), it is likely that the updated political content of the items loading on the new Traditional Moralism factor, which now appears to have much in common with the strictly political New Left Philosophy and Revolutionary Tactics factors, is a major reason for the observed positive relationship.

The implications of these findings will be developed in greater detail in Chapter 4.

Summary

A 90-item questionnaire was constructed and given to 153 Columbia College freshmen in the fall of 1968. The items were based upon (1) earlier research on the F-scale and variants on it, (2) earlier research on the Mach scales, (3) new items believed to capture 1968 reflections of the underlying dimensions of the above scales, and (4) new items believed relevant to the values underlying New Left student protests.

Factor analytic techniques indicated that the items grouped into five categories. Partly because of the relationships of some of these scales to ones used in the past, three factors were identified on the basis of common items and conceptual similarity to previous research. These were:

Traditional Moralism, which taps a conservative, status quo view of society, emphasizing traditional values about the worth of hard work, antipathy to new ideas, and the necessity of maintaining order—by the use of police force if necessary.

Machiavellian Tactics, which measures the extent to which individuals agree with a nonideological here-and-now philosophy of pragmatism and embrace the use of flattery, lying, and other techniques in interpersonal manipulation.

Machiavellian Cynicism, which implies a pessimistic belief in people and the existing social order.

Two new scales were developed:

New Left Philosophy, which may best be described as measuring the individual's disillusionment with the impact of modern society and endorsing the belief that although man is basically good, society has corrupted him.

Revolutionary Tactics, which reflects a complete loss of faith in existing social institutions and approval of violent measures to achieve change.

3

Methodology

This chapter reviews the methods of data collection and the characteristics of the samples that provided data for this book. Although the research began (inadvertently) with the administration of attitude scales to a psychology class at Columbia in the fall of 1967 and with our involvment in a study of participants in the Columbia demonstrations that spring, the major thrust of the research program was not initiated until the following fall. It continued until 1970. All samples described here were contacted during this 2-year period. Except where indicated, the attitude questionnaire that was administered consisted of the 60 items comprising the five 12-item factor scales described in the previous chapter. It will be referred to as the New Left scale.

The Core Sample: Columbia Class of 1972

During the summer of 1968 we decided to examine the relation between political attitudes and participation in political activities. We planned to focus our efforts on a longitudinal study of the incoming class at Columbia.

THE ORIENTATION WEEK QUESTIONNAIRE: SEPTEMBER 1968

Our first concern was to gather data to be used as premeasures in studying changes in attitudes and behavior. We wanted to administer the scales as early as possible in the students' careers so as to reduce the influence of experiences at Columbia. Accordingly, each of the 700 freshmen registering at Columbia College in September 1968 received a copy of a questionnaire in his orientation packet, along with the usual information about extracurricular activities, course evaluation booklets, and schedules. A covering letter informed the recipient that the questionnaire concerned matters of interest to the student community and that it was part of a study in which some Columbia students had already participated. The confidentiality of the student's responses was assured, and an envelope was provided for return of the questionnaire. At the bottom of the cover page the respondent was asked to indicate whether or not he would be willing to continue in the study if further information were needed. This was done to gauge if there was enough enterest to make a panel study feasible. At that time no monetary payment was offered. Before distribution to the-freshmen, the questionnaires were numbered at the bottom of the first page. Because the orientation packets were assembled with the name of the recipient on the front, these numbers could later be used to identify respondents. After 1 week, reminder slips were sent to all freshmen whose completed questionnaires we had not received.

By the end of the first week of classes (2 weeks after the freshmen had received the questionnaires) 254 individuals had responded, a return rate of 36.3%. At this point no attempt was made to recruit additional respondents. Of the 254 responding, 63% indicated willingness to continue with the project.

The first section of the questionnaire (see Appendix C-1) dealt with the student's feelings about the possible goals of a university; these questions were adapted from a questionnaire being distributed at the same time to a general sample of the university (see Auger, Barton, & Maurice, 1969). This was followed by questions about the respondent's activities in high school (political and nonpolitical), the presidential candidates he supported, and his feelings, knowledge, and sources of information about the demonstrations at Columbia the previous spring.

FIRST ADMINISTRATION OF THE MEASURE OF
NEW LEFT IDEOLOGY, NOVEMBER 1968

In mid-November 1968, we sent letters to the 254 students who had responded to the orientation week questionnaire, asking them to come to the Department of Social Psychology on any of three specified days to fill out additional questionnaires. They were told they would receive $3 for approximately 1½ hours of their time. These letters were mailed to the 254 freshmen regardless of whether they had or had not indicated a willingness to participate further, because we felt the monetary incentive might encourage those who had previously been uninterested.

When a subject arrived at the social psychology laboratory, he was given the original 90-item New Left Ideology scale to complete. Each respondent was identified by the last four digits of his social security number, which were matched with the numbers originally assigned to that respondent on the orientation week questionnaire.

After the initial 3-day testing period, we found that students with extreme political views, as measured by the candidate(s) they had supported in the presidential election on the orientation week questionnaire, were not well represented among the respondents. Therefore, a special effort was made to recruit such subjects, by calling all those who had indicated support for George Wallace, Ronald Reagan, Richard Nixon, Dick Gregory, or Eldridge Cleaver. By the end of the first week of December, 153 (60%) of the original 254 freshmen had responded. Data from this 153-member sample are used for some analyses discussed in the book, although the majority of data analyses of the Columbia Class of 1972 are based on the 122-member panel sample described in the following section.

SECOND ADMINISTRATION OF THE QUESTIONNAIRE
AND SCALE, DECEMBER 1969

During the first week in December 1969, approximately 1 year after the first administration of the New Left scale, data for the second wave of the panel were gathered. Each of the 153 students, then sophomores, was sent a letter asking him to come to the Department of Social Psychology to complete questionnaires similar to those he had filled out the previous year. Again we offered $3 as payment. Each subject was given the New Left scale (a shortened, 60-item version of the 90-item attitude scale he had taken as a freshman) and a "student questionnaire."

The "student questionnaire" was a four-page updated version of the orientation week questionnaire (see Appendix C-2). As before, there were questions about participation in political activities, both on and off the campus. This questionnaire also asked for background information—home town, parents' education levels, parents' political activity—and included general questions pertaining to changes in political interests during the past year.

Following the 3-day period, we attempted to recruit all subjects who had not returned; phone calls were made and letters were sent. Our final response rate was 79%, or 122 of the 153. Since 13 of the 153 had failed to register at Columbia for their sophomore year, the actual rate is 87%; only 18 of the possible 140 subjects did not return for the second wave of the panel. All subsequent analyses for the freshman panel sample are based on these 122 subjects (see especially Chapters 8 and 9). Their attitude scale scores, described in subsequent chapters, are composed of only the 60 items on which data from both freshman and sophomore years were gathered.

CHECKS ON THE REPRESENTATIVENESS OF THE SAMPLE

Through the efforts of the office of the Dean of Columbia College, a statistical description of the class of 1972 on a limited number of variables was made available to us. These data enabled us to compare the 122-member panel sample with their classmates. As can be seen in Table 3.1, the two groups are quite similar in most respects. There are, however, two significant deviations. First, a higher percentage of the class as a whole, as compared to panel members, reported themselves undecided about career plans. The difference is likely artifactual, since responses for the nonpanel members were taken from questionnaires completed the June prior to their freshman year, while those for the panel are answers given during orientation week. In the intervening 3 months, students were probably making tentative decisions about their careers. Second, the mean score on the mathematics scholastic aptitude test for panel members was 20 points higher than that for the remaining members of the class. However the mean scores on the verbal test are equal, and we have no obvious explanation for this difference.

Comparisons of the panel were also made with three other groups of Columbia students who had taken the orientation week questionnaire and the 90-item measure of New Left ideology in the autumn of 1968: (1) the 18 who returned to Columbia in 1969 but did not participate in the second (sophomore year) wave, (2) the 13 who did not return to Columbia in 1969, and (3) the 101 who failed to take the 90-item attitude scale later in the fall of 1968. The relevant data are found in Table 3.2. Neither the group of students who dropped out of school nor those who did not complete the forms as sophomores appear to differ substantially from the panel sample on measures of political values and behaviors. Only 3 of the possible 34 mean comparisons reach even marginal significance.

The dropouts, however, have one rather provocative characteristic—a very low variance on the Traditional Moralism scale. Not only is it significantly different from that of our panel sample ($F=3.49$, $df=121, 12$; $p<.01$), but it is also the lowest of any of our other college samples (e.g., New York University, Oregon State University, Fordham School of Social Work, etc.), and remarkably, although not surprisingly, similar to the variance of Traditional Moralism scores for a Berkeley counterculture group, who were also college dropouts (see Table 3.3). Although these 13 subjects represent only a small sample of those who dropped out of Columbia College, the finding makes a great deal of intuitive sense. Since scarcely anyone flunks out of Columbia, most of these students probably left voluntarily, a step which, regardless of specific political beliefs, represents a break from conventional ideas and expectations. As such, we would expect low scores and small variance in their scores on a measure of adherence to the status quo, i.e., the Traditional Moralism scale.

The 101 individuals who completed the first questionnaire during orientation week but did not return to complete the New Left scale constitute the group that is statistically least similar to the panel, although the discrepancies are not large. There are fewer activists among them and a significantly higher proportion supporting the liberal and reform presidential candidates than among the panel

Table 3.1
Comparison of Panel Sample with Entire Columbia Class of 1972

	Panel (N=122)	Remaining members of class[a] (N=578)
Geographical distribution (in percentages)		
East	71	75
South	7	5
Midwest	12	10
West	7	7
Foreign	3	2
Type of secondary school attended (in percentages)		
Public	73	68
Private and parochial	27	32
Probable career (in percentages)[b]		
Undecided	30	47
Medicine	17	12
Law	14	14
Scientific research	9	7
Teaching	11	11
Journalism	2	3
Business	3	3
Architecture	1	1
Engineering	2	2
Scholastic Aptitude Tests		
Verbal (mean score)	677	679
Math (mean score)	705	689
Rate of "dropping-out" of college (in percentages)	28	24

[a]The data made available through the dean's office were based on the entire class of 1972, panel sample included. The statistics presented in this column, therefore, represent extrapolations we made based on our knowledge of characteristics of the panel sample.
[b]The career plans for panel members were self-reports on arrival at Columbia; for the remaining members of the class they were self-reports the spring prior to coming to Columbia.

members. However, these findings are not unexpected. The reader will recall that we specifically tried to recruit those with extreme political positions when gathering subjects to take the New Left scale in the fall of 1968. These differences, therefore, are probably accounted for by the sampling procedures and were not entirely unanticipated.

Table 3.2
Comparison of the Panel Sample with Subsets of the Original Group of Columbia Freshmen

Freshman New Left scale scores	Panel (*N*=122)		Nonrespondents fall 1969 (*N*=18)		Not registered at Columbia fall 1969 (*N*=13)		Nonrespondents fall 1968 (*N*=101)
	$\bar{X}$	SD	$\bar{X}$	SD	$\bar{X}$	SD	
Traditional Moralism	2.88	1.06	3.03	1.10	2.38[a]	.57	—
Machiavellian Tactics	3.49	.85	3.05	.97	3.34	.81	—
Machiavellian Cynicism	3.73	.96	4.14	.94	4.02	1.08	—
New Left Philosophy	3.69	1.05	4.24[a]	1.29	3.84	.91	—
Revolutionary Tactics	2.65	1.00	2.85	1.47	3.01	1.18	—
Political activity before coming to Columbia (in percentages)							
Dissident activists	34		50		23		19[b]
Sympathizers	27		22		31		37
Nonactivists	39		28		46		44
Presidential candidate choice (in percentages)[c]							
Establishment	29		28		23		22
Liberal, reform	52		50		31		65[b]
Radical	14		17		31		11
Intended careers (in percentages)							
Law	15		11		—		16
Medicine	18		6		8		9[b]
Teaching	11		17		15		12
Science	11		6		8		15
Writer	7		—		15		1
Undecided	30		45		46		35
Other	8		15		8		12

[a] $.05 > p < .10$ between this sample and panel.
[b] $p < .05$ between the sample and panel.
[c] Percentages do not add to 100 because of respondents who reported supporting none of the candidates.

SUBSAMPLES OF THE PANEL

Friendship Study: Spring 1969. A study of the effects of political attitudes on friendship patterns was conducted by one of the authors between March and May of 1969, using as subjects 24 of the 153 Columbia freshmen.[1] The results of this study are discussed in Chapter 7. A snowball technique was used to obtain the sample—each person interviewed named other potential participants, who were subsequently interviewed and asked to give additional names.

The first stage involved interviewing 17 students with widely discrepant political views. They were chosen from the 153 freshmen on the basis of their scores on the New Left scale: 5 of the 10 most radical,[2] 5 of the 7 scoring at the mean, and the 7 most conservative. Each of these people was asked to give the names of all his "close friends" so as to provide the second stage of the snowball; their friends, in turn, were used for the third and final stage. Because of limitations of time and manpower, all the friends named could not be included; therefore, only one friend from each interviewee was randomly selected to be included in the study. In the instances where an individual was named by more than one person, an effort was made to interview him as well. No upperclassmen were included. The total number of students interviewed was 52; 19 were in the second and 16 in the third stage.

Each of the 52 respondents was contacted, by telephone, by one of the authors (a female) and asked to volunteer for a study of "friendship formation among freshmen" in which he would be interviewed for approximately 1 hour about his friends and what he was doing at Columbia. All but one (in the first stage) agreed to participate.

The interview was directed at the respondent's activities at Columbia and consisted of four sections: The first dealt with perceptions about Columbia, the second with the way his time was spent (e.g., how much time he spent studying, in extracurricular activities, etc.), the third with changes in himself—his attitudes and his perceptions—since coming to Columbia, and the fourth with his close friends at Columbia. This last section provided the meat of the interview, and most of the hour was devoted to it. At the end of the interview he was given a list of names and asked to indicate whom he knew and the extent of the friendship. This list consisted of the names of all the people in the friendship study at that time (i.e., the first stage of the snowball sample had a list of those in the first stage, the second stage had one containing those in the first and second stages, and so on).

The previous fall, and prior to the interview, 28 of the 52 subjects in the

---

[1] Students who had completed both parts of the first wave of the panel study.

[2] At first, the five most radical respondents were chosen as subjects, but three could not be reached and one refused to participate.

friendship study had not completed the New Left scale; they were given a shortened version of the scale which contained 20 items with the highest part-whole correlations (see Appendix B-1 for items). The split-half reliability of this shortened form for the 153 freshmen was .89. The subjects filled out the scale before being interviewed and did not discuss the questions on it with the interviewer. Since we hoped to use them for a panel study, the attitude scale was not readministered to the 24 subjects who were part of the original sample because retaking it could damage the validity of the larger study's results. We felt that significant changes in political attitudes from November to March could be ascertained during the interview.

Selected Interviews: Fall 1970. Rather than gather another wave of data from the entire panel sample the autumn of 1970, we decided to interview a small number of panel members to provide qualitative substance to the quantitative data.

The interviewing was done by a member of the Columbia College class of 1972 who was not a member of the panel but had worked as a research assistant helping to analyze the panel data. Since he was of the same age and sex, and came from the same milieu as the sample members, we felt he would be able to establish greater rapport with most respondents than could the authors.

Thirteen interviews were conducted, each interviewee drawn from one of thirteen groups into which we had divided the sample. Subjects had been assigned to these groups according to three criteria—activity in high school (three groups), initial scores on the Revolutionary Tactics scale (high or low), and, within these six groups, degree of radicalization from 1968 to 1969 as measured by proportional change on the Revolutionary Tactics scale. Previous analyses of the data had shown these groups to be meaningful (see Chapters 8 and 9).

In selecting interviewees from their respective groups, we tried to pick those individuals whom we felt typified the pattern of the group in terms of their scores on the five factor scales of the New Left scale, the nature of their political activity while at Columbia, their hometown, education of their parents, and so forth. The subject we felt to be most typical of each group was then called by the interviewer. He was told that he had been specifically selected to be interviewed about the development of his political beliefs as part of the study he had been participating in for the previous 2 years. Only one of these students could not be reached, and the individual designated as the second choice for that group had to be called. All those contacted agreed to be interviewed.

The interviews took place during the last week of October and the first 10 days of November; they were tape-recorded, and notes were not taken by the interviewer during the sessions. When the subject arrived, he was assured of the confidentiality of his responses. The interviewer then explained the purpose of the interview: to attempt to determine how political attitudes develop and change. The concern was not only with strictly political events but also with the philosophical, moral, and religious influences that might have affected the type and extent of the respondent's political involvement. After the explanation, the tape recorder was turned on. The interviews ranged from 50 to 75 minutes, averaging about 60 minutes. There were five sections in the interview: (1) changes in the student's political beliefs, political participation, and life style since his arrival at Columbia as a freshman, (2) the relationship between his attitudes and those of his parents and siblings, (3) his political attitudes and philosophy while in junior and senior high school and what (teachers, friends, events, etc.) he felt had influenced him during those years, (4) specific changes in politics while at Columbia, what caused them, and his reactions to certain recent events and cultural phenomena, and (5) his feelings about the future— what he wanted to do and what he thought he would do with his life.

Throughout, the interviewer guided the conversations toward topics concerned with the development of the subject's political awareness. He accepted what the subject said, but also probed for specifics, for example, what exactly he thought had made him change his ideas at that time, what kind of behavior he would engage in and why, and so on. If the subject answered questions only with generalities, he was asked about the impact on him of specific events—the 1968 Democratic Convention, living in Columbia dormitories, the 1970 invasion of Cambodia—or about changes in specific attitudes—cynicism, pragmatism, idealism.

Although the interviewer never disparaged any person's point of view, at times he would respond to answers by giving some of his own opinions. The respondents recognized this and when questioned after the interview commented that they did not feel it had inhibited or modified the expression of their own ideas. Some indeed believed the technique had brought out important points that perhaps otherwise would not have been articulated.

Additional Samples

Although our primary concern was to understand the core samples of Columbia students, responses from other samples were important in helping place the Columbia sample in perspective. Ideally, we would have liked to choose samples that allowed us to determine which parameters of the original sample could be generalized (for example, by gathering data from a comparable elite school on the West Coast or a comparable girls' school). Unfortunately, this was not possible. While we made a concerted effort to get groups that we thought would represent extreme attitudes (e.g., New York City policemen, self-proclaimed revolutionists), most of the additional samples were collected where we had contacts or where other researchers indicated an interest in the New Left scale.

SAMPLES GIVEN ORIGINAL FORM OF THE NEW LEFT SCALE

In Chapter 2 we discussed the fact that two forms of the 60-item scale were used in the research. About one-half of the additional samples received the form with the original item wordings, developed from the Columbia sample, while the other half received the revised version. This section describes the samples that took the original version. The scale scores, political activity of respondents, and demographic data are summarized in Table 3.3.

Community Colleges: Suffolk and Corning. Two former graduate students from the Columbia Social Psychology program who were teaching at community colleges in New York state were asked to administer the scale and background questionnaires to their introductory psychology classes. In each case one-half of the sample was given the original form of the scale, the other half took the revised version. This procedure was followed in order to give us the opportunity to compare systematically the two scales. The questionnaires were completed during a class period. All students complied with the request, and responses were anonymous. (See Appendix B-2b for an analysis of scores from the two versions.)

Oregon State University. A psychology professor from Oregon State University was interested in administering the New Left scale to his classes. The scales were sent to him and completed by his students during class time. A copy of the punched data cards was sent to us. To our knowledge, there were no refusals and all responses were anonymous.

Parents of Members of the Columbia Panel Sample. Immediately following the 1970 spring semester, a letter was sent to each of the 122 Columbia College students in the panel sample asking whether he would object to his parents completing the attitude scale. Enclosed in the letter was a postcard to be returned only if the student did not want the questionnaire sent to his parents. In mid-June two copies of the New Left scale accompanied by an explanatory letter were mailed to each set of parents.[3] The letter informed the parents that their son had been participating in a 2-year study of political attitudes and had given us permission to ask them to fill out the enclosed questionnaire. In the letter we discussed issues relating to the generation gap, stressing the lack of adequate research in the field. No monetary payment was offered, and responses

---

[3] We received postcards from 10 of the 122 students (8%) requesting us not to send the questionnaires to their parents. We also did not send the scales to one family living in Australia because of return postage problems—making a total of 11 sets of parents who were never contacted.

Table 3.3

Summary of Data from Samples That Completed the Original Form of the (Sixty-Item) New Left Scale[a]

Sample	Date given	N	Traditional Moralism		Machiavellian Tactics		Machiavellian Cynicism	
			$\bar{X}$	SD	$\bar{X}$	SD	$\bar{X}$	SD
Columbia	Fall 1968	122	2.88	1.06	3.49	.85	3.73	.96
panel	Fall 1969	122	2.85	.95	3.38	.75	3.87	.82
Suffolk Community College	Spring 1969	33	3.37	.85	3.65	.70	3.97	.93
Corning Community College	Spring 1969	33	3.22	.89	3.46	.58	3.71	.65
Oregon State University	Fall 1969	134	3.39	.76	3.45	.77	3.52	.70
Parents of Columbia panel	Summer 1970	165	3.53	.92	3.22	.79	3.16	.77
Berkeley counter-culture	Summer 1970	31	1.95	.57	2.73	.69	4.83	.69
New York City police	Summer and Fall 1970	23	4.00	.76	3.73	.67	2.93	.55
Construction workers	Fall 1970	20	4.02	—	4.00	—	3.17	—
Yankelovich–CBS national survey	Spring 1969	747			3.58	.70[e]		

[a]A dash indicates no data available.

[b]For the criteria used in classifying activities, see Appendix D. A member of the parents of Columbia panel sample was considered an activist if he or she had engaged in any type of organized political activity (i.e., Democratic or Republican party work as well as less conventional activity such as foreign resistance work during World War II).

[c]Based on own educational level, not that of fathers.

[d]Approximate average age.

[e]Based on a 15-item scale (see Appendix B-3).

Table 3.3 (continued)

New Left Philosophy		Revolutionary Tactics		Percentage of activists[b]	Percentage of males	Mean age	Percentage of fathers who graduated college	Percentage stating own religion as "none"
$\bar{X}$	SD	$\bar{X}$	SD					
3.69	1.05	2.65	1.00	34	100	18	59	–
3.82	1.10	3.07	1.09	79	100	19	59	–
3.90	.78	2.80	.74	16	52	21	18	30
3.92	.77	2.79	.78	22	48	19	30	15
3.77	.82	2.73	.72	–	57	20	45	–
3.45	.83	2.02	.62	20	45	–	64[c]	–
5.09	.79	5.45	.97	100	55	22	–	–
3.28	.75	2.15	.62	–	100	32[d]	–	–
3.63	–	2.85	–	0	100	30[d]	–	–
				42	56	20	–	17

were voluntary. Each parent was also urged not to discuss the attitude question with his or her spouse.

Two follow-up requests were sent. The first, in mid-July, was merely a reminder note; the second contained a return postcard on which the parents could check whether they were still planning to fill out the questionnaire, were unwilling to complete it, or wanted additional copies. This last request was mailed at the beginning of August, and analysis of the data began at the end of that month.

Completed attitude scales were received from at least one member of 93 of the

111 families to which forms had been mailed. Table 3.4 presents a comparison of respondents and nonrespondents with respect to relevant demographic variables reported by their sons on the questionnaires filled out at Columbia (see Appendix C-2). The two groups are remarkably similar. The only significant difference between them is in relation to the sons' reports of the political activity of the mothers. Nonrespondents were less likely than respondents to have engaged in some sort of organized political endeavor ($X^2=6.39$, $df=1$; $p<.05$). The same trend is seen for fathers, but the difference is not significant. Such a bias is not totally unexpected. Parents who are interested in politics (and evidence it by virtue of their political participation) are likely to be more willing to complete a questionnaire concerned with such matters than those not so interested.

Table 3.4

Comparison of Responding and Nonresponding Parents of Panel Members, by Educational Level, Political Activity, and Demographic Factors (Expressed in Percentages)[a]

	Respondents (N=93)		Nonrespondents (N=29)	
	Mother (N=90)	Father (N=75)	Mother (N=32)	Father (N=47)
Education				
High school graduate or less	27	21	24	34
Some college	49	31	56	34
Some graduate school	22	46	20	32
Political participation				
Active	39	39	12	25
Inactive	61	61	88	75
Region of country				
Northeast	70		76	
South	7		7	
Midwest	10		10	
West	10		0	
Foreign	1		7	
Hometown (USA)				
New York City and suburbs	42		58	
Cities over 1,000,000 and their suburbs	17		10	
Cities 200,000-1,000,000	17		17	
Cities under 200,000	23		10	

[a]Where percentages do not add to 100 it is because of rounding and respondents not answering.

Berkeley Counterculture Group. A question raised by some of our more radical young critics was the extent to which our Columbia radicals were typical of truly revolutionary dissidents. After all, they were still officially enrolled in college, which might indicate less than full commitment to radical activities.

In the summer of 1970 it was possible to collect data on individuals in Berkeley, California, who were known to be participants in protest activities. There were two stipulations for inclusion of respondents in this sample: (1) They had to have attended college and to have left (by self-report) for ideological reasons and (2) they had to identify themselves as self-styled revolutionaries as well as be known by others to be involved in the counterculture. It is, of course, impossible to estimate how representative this group is of any New Left populations, but, for the purpose of drawing comparisons with other groups, our interest was primarily in individuals who were clearly dissident.

The data were collected by a 1968 leader of the Columbia SDS who had spent the subsequent 2 years in a variety of legal and illegal protest activities. Respondents were approached individually, and roughly one-half of them completed the forms. Possible sources of bias could not be determined.

Usable protocols were returned by 31 individuals: 17 male, 14 female. Ages ranged from 18 to 31, the length of college attendance varied from one semester in college to 2 years in a graduate or professional school, and the median length of time since leaving school was roughly 2 years. There was wide variation in the kinds of schools attended, from community colleges to Ivy League schools, and the group had a diverse regional background.

New York City Police. The 23 members of the New York City Police Department who completed the form were from two undergraduate classes in a required economics course at the John Jay College of the City University of New York. The classes averaged about 30 in size and included students other than members of the Police Department. The regular instructor asked that only policemen volunteer to fill out the forms; those so volunteering filled them out at home and returned them by mail to Columbia University. There is no way of estimating the possible effects of volunteer bias.

Attendance at John Jay was voluntary on the part of the policemen. Reasons for taking the course varied; some officers wanted a college degree to enhance post-retirement job opportunities (they could retire after 20 years of service), some were merely intellectually curious, others felt that the courses would be of assistance in taking examinations for advancement within the Police Department. It is highly probable that the self-selection involved in attending college indicated that the respondents were more intellectually curious and ambitious than those not taking advantage of such opportunities, but this is only speculative.

The respondents ranged in age from 25 to 40, with an average age of about 32. Since they were all on active duty, the minimum income was $10,000 a year. All were male. Ethnic background was not asked, but the instructor's estimate is that about one-sixth of the police students were black and the rest primarily of Irish and Italian backgrounds.

Construction Workers. Twenty members of an elevator construction union completed the scales. They were all Caucasian and primarily of Irish origin. The scales were adminstered in a class in elevator repair required of all union members and given by an instructor who was himself a union member. This class was one of many that the union provides for its workers. Seven of the 20 did not answer all questions, and their scores were prorated on the basis of items completed.

Ages ranged from 21 to 37, with 10 respondents being 30 years of age or older, 3 respondenis had failed to complete high school, 10 were high school graduates, and 6 had had some exposure to college. On a question about political activities, none acknowledged participating in antiwar protests, but 9 said they had been involved in a pro-Vietnam Wall Street rally of May 1970, when student protesters were attacked. There were no significant differences between those acknowledging participation in the latter event and those not. However, participants in the Wall Street demonstration tended to be younger, less educated, and more likely to omit answers on the questionnaire.

Yankelovich–CBS National Survey. During the spring of 1969, 747 college students were interviewed by Daniel Yankelovich, Inc., a private social science research firm, as part of a Columbia Broadcasting Service (CBS) survey on the political attitudes of youth. The students represented 30 schools selected at random from a nationwide list. The institutions ranged from well-known universities, such as Harvard and Berkeley, to relatively little-known schools, such as Rio Hondo Junior College, and included those with religious affiliations and high minority group representation. The number of respondents from each school varied from 12 to 39, but was not proportional to undergraduate enrollment. One school had 4 representatives and was eliminated from our analyses.

Respondents were contacted by a fellow student and interviewed in person, using a fixed schedule of eight typed pages. Interspersed throughout were fifteen items from our 90-item measure of New Left ideology. These items are presented in Appendix B-3. Unfortunately, the responses were not scored on a uniform scale; some were based on two alternatives (agree-disagree), some on three alternatives (strongly agree, partially agree, and disagree); none, however, were based on the 7-point response scale used by all other samples reported here. In order to obtain a summed attitude score comparable to the other data, the Yankelovich categories were weighted as if they had been based on a 7-point scale. "Strongly agree" was scored at 7, "agree" as 6, "partially agree" as 5, and "disagree" as 2.

SAMPLES GIVEN THE REVISED VERSION
OF THE NEW LEFT SCALE

This section describes the samples that took the revised version of the 60-item scale. The summarized data from these samples are found in Table 3.5.

Columbia College (Psychology Class). The revised 60-item scale was given to members of the introductory psychology class in the spring, 1969 as part of a course unit on personality. It was administered, along with additional scales measuring anxiety and neuroticism, by teaching assistants in the five laboratory sections, each of which had about 20 students. The laboratories were mandatory—work missed had to be made up—and thus they were well attended. One student refused to complete the questionnaire and the accompanying background questionnaire.

New York University (NYU). The New Left scale and a background questionnaire were also given in the introductory psychology course at NYU in the spring of 1969, but under different conditions than at Columbia. They were given in three large lecture classes of about 200 students each, for which attendance was not mandatory. When the forms were administered, only about one-third of the students were in class. Although we cannot accurately determine the representativeness of the students who completed the scale, it is our impression that they were not a random sample of the NYU introductory psychology class. The professors and some students reported that, in general, only students anxious to get an A or those who wanted to be sure of a B came to class regularly as well as those with academic problems who were afraid they might fail. It seems that a B was a guaranteed grade for the average student who did the reading but did not attend lectures. Thus, the NYU sample is probably a heterogeneous one, representing a bimodal distribution of academic standing. Inclement weather on the first day of testing, when two of the three sections met, perhaps also contributed to the low attendance. However, all students who did attend class completed the questionnaires, and responses were anonymous.

Community Colleges: Suffolk and Corning. (See under "Samples Given Original Form of the New Left Scale.")

Private School Faculty. Teachers at a private progressive high school located near Harlem in New York City constituted another sample. Some members of the Department of Social Psychology at Columbia designed a questionnaire

Table 3.5
Summary of Data from Samples That Completed the Revised Form of the Sixty-Item New Left Scale[a]

Sample	Date given	N	Traditional Moralism		Machiavellian Tactics		Machiavellian Cynicism	
			X	SD	X	SD	X	SD
Columbia College (psychology class)	Spring 1969	110	2.39	.92	3.38	.91	4.16	.80
New York U.	Spring 1969	214	2.90	.96	3.43	.78	4.25	.82
Suffolk Community College	Spring 1969	35	3.24	.85	3.69	.82	4.32	.87
Corning Community College	Spring 1969	33	3.10	.83	3.26	.72	3.97	.76
Private school faculty	Spring 1969	51	2.67	.71	3.01	.74	3.89	.89
Fordham School of Social Work	Fall 1969	161	3.08	.94	3.08	.82	3.88	.72
New York State Employment counselors	Summer 1970	39	2.41	.80	3.13	.86	4.10	.80
New York City adults	Summer 1970	151	3.03	1.08	3.58	.89	4.14	.76
High school students	Spring 1970	195					3.40	

[a]A dash indicates data not available.
[b]For the criteria used in classifying activists, see Appendix D.
[c]Based on own educational level, not that of fathers.
[d]Based on a 30-item scale.

concerning faculty opinion about teaching practices and policy decisions for the school, and, in return the headmaster agreed to ask all faculty members to complete the New Left scale and some background questions. The faculty questionnaire and the New Left scale were both completed by 51 teachers at a faculty meeting in May 1969.

Fordham School of Social Work. A professor at the Fordham School of Social Work interested in research with the New Left scale administered the scale along with a lengthy questionnaire concerning social work as a career, knowledge of sociological phenomena, and the students' socioeconomic background. The questionnaire was given in September 1969, during the first meeting of a

Table 3.5 (continued)

New Left Philosophy		Revolutionary Tactics		Percentage of activists[b]	Percentage of males	Mean age	Percentage of fathers who graduated college	Percentage stating own religion as none
X	SD	X	SD					
4.17	1.00	3.71	1.21	64	100	20	73	45
4.01	.88	3.18	.86	33	51	19	39	36
3.71	.78	2.88	.65	14	66	21	29	14
3.87	.73	3.19	.68	18	42	19	42	18
3.81	.91	3.33	.96	59	33	35	100[c]	57
3.70	.87	3.32	.71	32	29	28	21	20
4.00	.98	3.34	.75	–	–	–	–	–
4.04	1.02	3.26	.90	–	46	38	45[c]	11
.72[d]				21	43	17	41	–

required introductory course in research methods. All first-year entering students in the social work school as well as a few second-year students who had not taken the course the previous year completed the questionnaire. Unlike respondents in the other samples, these respondents were asked to sign their names.

New York State Employment Counselors. During the summer of 1970, a group of employment counselors of the New York State Employment Service were given a course in attitudes, which they were required to pass to maintain their counseling positions. As part of the classwork, each was asked to complete the scale during class time. No one refused, and all responses were anonymous.

New York City Adults. One of the assignments for the class of employment counselors was to find four people to complete the New Left scale. Rather than selecting four friends, the counselors were required to recruit a female and a

Table 3.6
Description of Respondents from Different Classes in the High School Sample

	Number of males	Number of females	Percentage that refused to participate	Percentage return rate	Mean item score on New Left scale	SD	Percentage of activists	Percentage of fathers with more than high school education
Tenth grade	34	36	–	–	3.51	.60	20	57
Eleventh grade	23	43	4	80	3.38	.83	23	56
Twelfth grade	26	34	11	67	3.28	.73	20	72

male who had not graduated from high school, and a male and a female with some graduate or professional education. To further extend the heterogeneity of the sample, the ages of the respondents were to be as varied as possible. The counselors noted the age, sex, education, religion, and political party preference of each respondent. We have no measure of refusal rate, but presumably this sample was made up of voluntary respondents. All responses were anonymous.

High School Students. The high school respondents came from one of two high schools in a suburban Long Island community that is new and rapidly growing (population approximately 16,000 in 1960, and 25,230 in 1970). The median income of the town in 1969 was $10,000, the percentage of whites 98.6. The reasons for choosing this particular school were purely pragmatic; it was the only one to which we could obtain ready access. We had approached the administration of a high school in a more urban and heterogeneous community for permission to give the scales but had been refused because of problems with parents over prior research in that school system.

The sample was gathered by two means. Using class lists, one out of every five eleventh- and twelfth-grade students was called on the phone by a member of the twelfth-grade class of the school. The student was asked if he or she would participate in a research project by completing a short attitude questionnaire, for which he or she would be paid $1. If a subject refused, the next person on the list was called. The questionnaire and a return envelope were then mailed to each student who had agreed to participate. The tenth-grade data were collected by a social studies teacher, who gave the forms to her three sections of sophomore students during class time. Since all tenth graders, except those in the honors program, were assigned randomly to social studies sections, we assume this sample to be fairly unbiased.

The questionnaire was divided into two parts: background information and the attitude scale. The background sheets included questions about age, year in school, college plans, parental education level, and political participation. The attitude scale given to the high school students was a shortened version of the revised New Left scale. It comprised 30 items, most of which had part-whole correlations greater than .30 on the original scale given to the basic Columbia freshman sample. The scale consisted of 11 items from New Left Philosophy, 10 from Revolutionary Tactics, 6 from Traditional Moralism, and 3 from the two Machiavellian scales. (See footnote to Appendix B-2a for items used.)

Table 3.6 presents additional characteristics of the sample. We found no differences between males and females, nor among sophomores, juniors, and seniors on either ideology or activity measures. However, there were differences in return rates. Seniors were less likely than juniors to return the questionnaires once they had been mailed to them (and more likely to refuse to fill them out when first called); the same pattern was found for males as opposed to females.

4

Ideology and Behavior:
The Protester's Profile

A continuing problem in attitudinal research has been the relation between how an individual responds on a paper-and-pencil questionnaire, in an interview, or to projective techniques, and what he actually does in relevant situations. Since our research relied heavily on the use of questionnaires, that is, the attitude scales described in the second chapter, we looked to behavioral measures to validate self-reported beliefs. This chapter describes the relationship of scale scores to self-report of political protest behavior and to membership in various groups.

The data initially used to test these relationships come from a sample of 153 Columbia freshmen, class of 1972, the core sample cited throughout most of the book. The findings were striking, and as a result we examined other college and noncollege groups to check on their generalizability. First we present the data from the Columbia freshmen.

The Classification of Respondents by Protest Activity

A questionnaire filled out by the freshmen during orientation week in September 1968 included questions about precollege activities relating to protest against the Vietnam War and civil rights matters. Responses to these items enabled us to classify individuals into three groups. (The questions on which this classification was based are in Appendix D.) Except where indicated, respondents in the other samples were divided according to identical criteria.

Nonactivists: These individuals reported they had not engaged in any activities in support of war protest or civil rights.

Sympathizers: These individuals reported they had signed petitions, contributed money, tutored ghetto children, and otherwise actively supported peace and civil rights activities; however, they had not engaged in behavior that represented direct or potentially direct confrontation with authority.

Dissident activists: These individuals reported they had participated in peace marches, picketing, sit-ins, voter registration, or other acts that in a sense "put their body on the line."

New Left Ideology and Activism in the Basic Columbia Sample

Before examining the relationship of protest behavior to the individual factor scales, we analyzed the relationship of the behavior to the global measure of New Left ideology from the original 90-item scale. (This measure consisted of the summed score on the 62 new items we had devised.) The 153 freshmen in the sample had completed this scale in the fall of their first semester at college. The scores of the members of each of the three activity groups are shown graphically in Figure 4.1. The overall relation between attitudes and behavior is

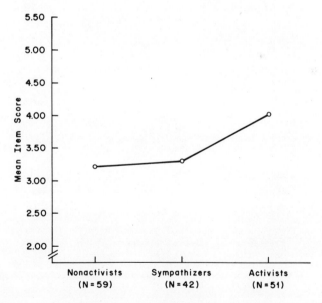

Figure 4.1. New Left ideology scores of Columbia freshman sample by degree of precollege activism. (Data on 152 of the 153 freshmen were available.)

highly significant (*F*=21.80; *df*=2,149, *R*<.01). The figure indicates, moreover, that it is the activist students who account for the major part of the relationship.

We used the orientation week questionnaire to look at the relationship between endorsement of New Left ideology and choice of presidential candidates. These choices were particularly salient at this time (mid-September 1968), following as they did the involvement of students in the McCarthy primaries in the spring, the assassination of Robert Kennedy in June, and the climactic events at the Democratic Convention in Chicago less than a month prior to the beginning of the academic year.

Members of the sample were presented with a list of the prominent presidential candidates and asked to indicate those whom they had favored at any time for president. This procedure permitted them to check as many names as they wished, the rationale being that supporters of Reagan or Rockefeller might have switched to Nixon after his nomination; Kennedy, Johnson, or McCarthy supporters might have opted for Humphrey after he received the Democratic nomination, and so on. Five groupings emerged and are used as indicators of presidential preference in Figure 4.2.

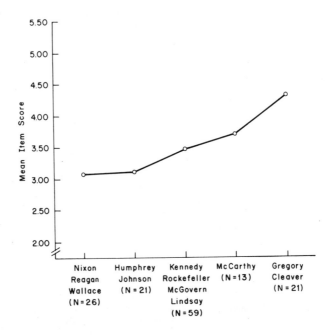

Figure 4.2. New Left ideology scores of Columbia freshman sample by presidential candidate preference (1968).

Not surprisingly, the relationship between New Left ideology and presidential preference is highly significant (F=17.49; df=4,135, R<.01). Perhaps the most interesting finding is the lack of differentiation on the New Left scale among preferences for candidates who were at the time basically hawkish on Vietnam—Nixon, Reagan, Wallace, Johnson, and Humphrey.

The relationship between attitudes and a combined index of presidential preference and activity was also examined. In this analysis a three-way break on presidential preference was used—lumping supporters of Nixon and Humphrey together, putting the "only McCarthy" supporters with those in favor of Rockefeller, McGovern, Kennedy, and McCarthy as a moderate group, and leaving the Cleaver and Gregory supporters to hold the radical bastion. "Purified" activity groups were created by including in the nonactivist group only those subjects who supported Nixon or Humphrey, in the sympathizer group only those who supported the moderate candidates, and in the dissident activist group only those who supported Cleaver and Gregory. When limiting the sample to these respondents, the relationship between protest activity and scores on the New Left scale becomes markedly accentuated (see Figure 4.3).

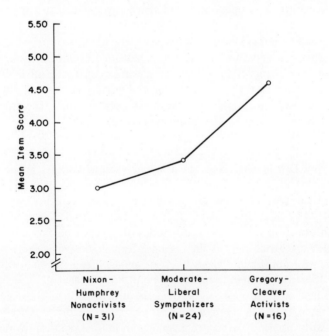

Figure 4.3. New Left ideology scores of Columbia freshman sample by activity groups, "purified" by presidential preference.

New Left Ideology and Activism in a High School Sample

The high degree of precollege activism (30%) of the panel sample surprised us, and we wondered at what age participation in political protest and the endorsement of the New Left beliefs typically began. In an attempt to investigate this question we obtained access to a high school sample from a predominantly white middle-class community on Long Island. The data were collected in the spring of 1970 just before the Cambodian invasion and the Jackson State College and Kent State University killings. For reasons of time and economy, only 30 items were chosen from the revised form of the scale, with its simpler wording. Since there are no differences in the proportion of activists or in attitude scores among members of the sophomore, junior, or senior classes, the scores of students from all three classes have been combined for this analysis.

For this sample, only two questions were used to classify level of protest activity. The first was whether the student had worked in any group that had tried to change school policy; the second was whether the student had participated in any antiwar demonstrations. Those answering both questions in the negative were classified nonactivists, those involved in school policy changes only were classified sympathizers, and those participating in antiwar protests (whether or not they also reported, as did most, participation in attempted changes of school policy) were classified dissident activists.

The relationship between New Left item mean scores and activism is shown in Figure 4.4. The shape of the curve and the mean attitude scores of the three groups are similar to those found in the Columbia panel sample although the attitude items and the criteria for activism had been modified. The proportion of activists, however, is lower—21% as opposed to 30%.

New Left Ideology and Activism in a National College Sample

Some of the attitude items that we had developed were used in a national survey of 747 college students conducted by Daniel Yankelovich for the background information of a CBS special series of telecasts on the generation gap. Although Yankelovich altered the response format somewhat, we were able to use responses from the interviews to create an ideology index that was based on a sum of 15 items weighted to reflect a 7-point Likert scale.

Respondents were also asked questions about their political activity, but these again differed from the ones used with our college samples. Often they did not deal with specific events or were ambiguous in their political relevance. Only those items that could be directly identified as protest-related were considered in our analysis. For example, a question about being "arrested" was not used since it did not specify whether arrest was caused by illegal political activity, speeding,

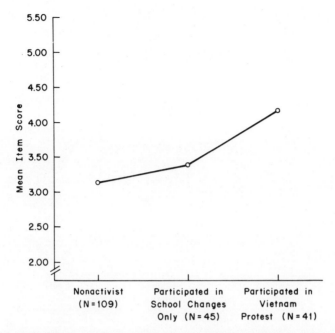

Figure 4.4. Abbreviated New Left scale scores by reported political activity among high school students. (Based on a 30-item version of the New Left scale.)

possession of drugs, or any of a variety of other reasons. An index of political activism was derived by summing the number of activities in which an individual had participated, weighting confrontation events twice as much as nonconfrontation ones. (The items used and the scoring system are included in Appendix D.)

Differences in the items used and in the classification of activities prevent us from comparing the Yankelovich data directly with our own. Crucial to the present analysis, however, is the relationship between the index of New Left orientation and self-reported political activism. The correlation is .53 ($p<.01$ level). Estimates of reliability of these measures are extremely hazardous, so we will content outselves with noting that, using derived measures, the relationship between self-reported protest activity and ideology again comes through loud and clear.

The Five Scales and Activism

The five scales derived from the factor analysis of the original pool of 90 items show a complex set of interrelationships (see Chapter 2). They are also significantly related to protest behavior. In Figure 4.5, mean item scores on each of

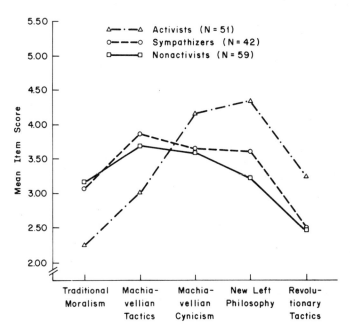

Figure 4.5. New Left scale scores of Columbia freshman sample by degree of precollege activism.

the five factor scales obtained from the 153 Columbia freshmen in November 1968 are plotted against the degree of precollege activism as reported on the orientation week questionnaire.

In this comparison, the first inklings of what we call the "protester's profile" emerge. Dissidents score significantly lower than sympathizers and nonactivists on Traditional Moralism and Machiavellian Tactics, but significantly higher on Machiavellian Cynicism, New Left Philosophy, and Revolutionary Tactics. When the scale scores are plotted against the activity groups purified by presidential preference, as shown in Figure 4.6, these relationships are stronger.

Generality of the Profile

Scores on the five scales, self-statements of protest activity, and other background information were obtained from six additional samples during 1969. The samples were:

1. The entire class of the spring semester introductory psychology course at Columbia College. Most respondents were sophomores. (N=110)

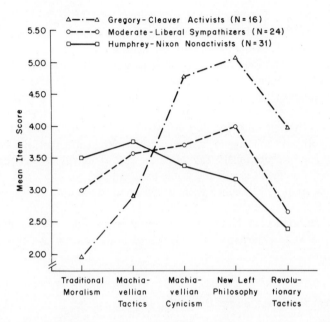

Figure 4.6. New Left scale scores of Columbia freshman sample by activity groups, "purified" by presidential preference.

2. All students attending class sessions late in the spring semester of the introductory psychology course at the Washington Square campus of New York University. (N=214)
3. Two classes in introductory psychology at Corning Community College. (N=67)
4. Two classes in introductory psychology at Suffolk Community College. (N=67)
5. Almost the entire teaching staff of a private elementary and secondary school in New York City. (N=51)
6. All first-year students at the Fordham School of Social Work. (N=161)

All of these samples took the revised form of the scale except for the community college psychology classes, where half took the original and half the revised form of the scale. The mean scores for these two samples on each of the scales have been averaged across the two forms because no significant differences were found between the forms for either school.

The percentage of self-proclaimed activists varied from 15% at one of the community colleges to 64% at Columbia. This may reflect individual predispositions to protest, but also reflects opportunities for engaging in protest. There were, as is obvious, differences in the availability of such activity in New York compared with Suffolk County, which was at the time predominantly Republican, nonurban, and not the site of any major protests.

Despite these variations, the same patterns on the five scales recurred. Dissident activists were uniformly and significantly lower on Traditional Moralism than sympathizers, who were lower still than those engaging in no political protest activity; the pattern on Machiavellian Tactics, of lower scores for activists and higher ones for nonactivists, was relatively consistent but not always significant; the higher scores on Machiavellian Cynicism, New Left Philosophy, and Revolutionary Tactics on the part of activists in these aggregates again were the same as those found in the basic sample.

This replication of relationships in samples with quite different demographic characteristics provides convincing evidence for a well-defined profile of individuals who reported participation in confrontation activities. They differed from their less active counterparts on measures of both political and interpersonal ideology.

Validity Check on the Use of Self-Reports

An obvious problem of this kind of research is the reliance placed on the self-report of protest activity. Although we have no formal check on political activity, at least for the Columbia sample we do have collaborative evidence from campus newspapers and from interviews in which students verbally confirmed what they had previously reported on the questionnaires. We also reasoned that by selecting samples whose life styles reflected their political stance and comparing them with college samples that shared similar political activity patterns, we would have more confidence in our data. Simultaneously this would allow us to generalize our findings to noncampus radicals and nonradicals. In the following section we report material collected from two groups viewed as antagonistic to student protesters—members of the New York City Police Department and elevator workers in the construction industry. The responses of these groups are counterposed against those of self-proclaimed revolutionaries living in Berkeley, California.

COMPARISONS OF SCORES OF IDEOLOGICALLY
OPPOSED GROUPS

In Figure 4.7, the scores on the five scales are plotted for each of these groups. The Berkeley radicals show the by-now-familiar profile of the protester, low on Traditional Moralism and Machiavellian Tactics, high on Machiavellian Cynicism and New Left Philosophy, and extremely high on Revolutionary Tactics. For

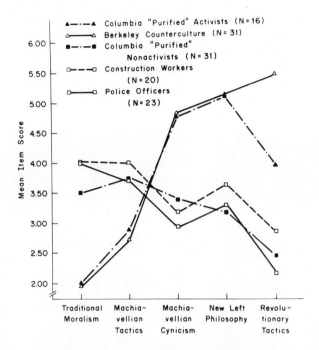

Figure 4.7. New Left scale scores among ideologically opposed groups.

comparative purposes the scores of the "purified" radical group of Columbia freshmen are plotted. The two curves are practically identical, not differing significantly except on Revolutionary Tactics. There are two possible reasons for the latter difference. The Berkeley data were collected in the summer of 1970, a later and more radical time than the fall of 1968, when the Columbia data were collected. Yankelovich (1969) noted increased radicalization among college students between October 1968, and the following spring, and it is quite likely that the trend continued for at least a year afterward, as the student protest spread from activist campuses to previously somnolent ones. The second factor is that the Berkeley group had felt strongly enough about their views to leave school and commit themselves to the "revolution" on a full-time basis, while the Columbia radicals had not left school.

The police and construction workers show an opposite profile from the Berkeley radicals and do not differ significantly from one another. Again, for comparative purposes, the scores of the Columbia freshmen conservatives are plotted. These college students, who had not participated in any protest and who supported Establishment candidates in the 1968 election, do not differ significantly from the police and construction workers on any of the scales.

Our interpretation of these data is straightforward. Although there may have been dissimulation on the part of respondents in reporting their own political activities, it was not sufficient to have a major effect on the results. The groups of self-proclaimed revolutionaries and those with known right-wing proclivities show, respectively, the same patterns of response as those college students we identified as radical activists and conservative nonactivists.

Discussion

The differing patterns on three of the scales, Traditional Moralism, New Left Philosophy, and Revolutionary Tactics, are what would be expected by anyone with knowledge of the content of the scales and familiarity with student protesters. Rebels are typically less in agreement with statements endorsing traditional moralistic values. For our samples, the greater their disagreement with these values, the greater the likelihood of their participating in political protest. It is likewise not surprising that the protesters and nonactivists differ on New Left Philosophy and Revolutionary Tactics. After all, the items in these scales were based upon statements broadcast and circularized by dissidents during the Columbia occupation; those with similar inclinations should agree with them.

The relationship between protest and scores on the Machiavellian Tactics and Machiavellian Cynicism scales was by far the most interesting pattern to emerge from the data. The dissident profile of being low on Tactics and high on Cynicism had not been predicted in advance. Fifteen years of research on Machiavellianism (or interpersonal manipulation) had not suggested such a relationship. Scores on the two scales had previously been positively correlated in many samples of college students, and the usual procedure had been to use combined scores (Machiavellian Tactics and Machiavellian Cynicism) as an over-all measure of Machiavellianism. However, Christie and Geis noted in 1970, "Our suspicion is that revolutions are not initiated by high Mach[iavellians] but by a subset of low or middle Mach[iavellians] who are capable of great moral indignation at the failure of the existing system and who by virtue of their affective involvement with a potentially new order crystallize opposition to the old one [p. 352]." The results summarized in this section indicate that the revolutionaries are indeed a subset of individuals who score in the middle of the distribution on the total Machiavellian scale; they score low on Tactics and high on Cynicism. But they differ from another subset of middle Machiavellians— the conservatives, who score high on Machiavellian Tactacs and relatively low on Cynicism.

New data supporting this relationship, as well as observations of and discussions with young dissidents, make this differential discrepancy, which seemed so novel when first encountered, self-evident in retrospect. Confrontation tactics involve "telling it like it is." The more traditional manipulative strategies—of compromise, of withholding the truth, of dissembling, of flattery—were emphatically rejected by militants of the New Left, just as the other perceived hypocrisies of American society were rejected by them. "People should be honest at all times," one of the Columbia sample members told us. He insisted that government officials and politicians should be honest, and he respected only those individuals, such as General Westmoreland, who he felt lived up to this ideal.

Concomitant with this belief was a highly cynical view of people in general, who were perceived as fallible and morally weak. As the protesters looked about, they saw their parents questioning their relationship to each other and dissatisfied with their careers. A typical reaction to this was: "I will try to do what I want to do, whereas my parents' lives have been dominated by necessity or compulsion." Such cynicism extended to their beliefs about the nature of society and the potential for its reform as well. No longer were the students surprised by events that outraged many citizens during the late 1960s—Robert Kennedy's assassination, the Mylai massacre, the Black Panther trials; they had come to expect these as necessary outgrowths of a political system they desperately wanted to change but did not believe to be amenable to change. As one activist put it: "I am waiting for something drastic to happen to unstatify (sic) the situation . . . [but] I don't think it will help." The pervasiveness of this pessimism was enormous. During the in-depth interviews of 13 members of the original Columbia sample at the start of their junior year, we asked if they had any idea what they would be doing in 25 or 30 years. "I'll probably be dead," was the spontaneous reply of several. They were 20 years old at the time.

One of the curious paradoxes of the New Left ideology is the juxtaposition of this cynicism about people and the almost Rousseauean idealization of man reflected in New Left Philosophy scores—man is basically good, but has been corrupted by the Establishment. The contradiction, however, is more apparent than real. The distrust revealed in the high Machiavellian Cynicism scores is based on a perception of people caught up in an intolerable society. The New Left Philosophy scale captures a more abstract notion—an idyllic vision of all mankind, which would be possible in utopian communities but is not a reality within the contemporary social framework.

Another puzzling aspect of New Left ideology is brought out in the oft-repeated statement of observers, "I agree with their goals but not their tactics." It seems that those making such remarks were also troubled by many of the ills that beset modern American society, such as the Vietnam War, the lagging progress in civil rights, environmental pollution, and the rest of the litany. However, we suggest that they were more accustomed to making accommodations within the system (use of Machiavellian tactics) and therefore could not easily understand the direct action, non-Machiavellian tactics, of the young. While many parents were horrified by the burning of draft centers, their children often sat undisturbed. A statement by one not particularly radical Columbia student is especially revealing: "I guess a meaningful political act for me would be anything from addressing political leaflets to bombings."

Summary

The relationship between scores on the New Left scale and reported involvement in political protest activity was examined in a wide variety of samples. As expected, respondents who had participated in potential confrontation situations (rallies, demonstrations, marches, etc.) were significantly more likely to be favorable toward the ideas of the New Left than were sympathizers or nonactivists. This difference was best seen when the measure of political activity was used in combination with preference for presidential candidates in the 1968 election. Protest activity was also found to be significantly related to scores on each of the five subscales. This pattern may be dubbed the "protester's profile." Radical activists and members of a group of Berkeley self-proclaimed revolutionaries scored low on Traditional Moralism and Machiavellian Tactics, and high on Machiavellian Cynicism, New Left Philosophy, and Revolutionary Tactics. Nonactivists, policemen, and construction workers exhibited the reverse pattern of scores.

5

Family Background and Protest Ideology

When we commenced research in 1968 we had no reason to doubt the general consensus among researchers that there were consistencies in the family backgrounds of student protesters. A few examples:

> Activists are found to be intellectually gifted, academically superior, and politically radical young people from advantaged homes in which their parents are successful in their careers, comfortable in their economic position, and liberal in their political orientations [Block, Haan, & Smith, 1969, p. 144].

> A major finding of the pioneering empirical research on the American student movement of the 1960's was that students who engaged in campus protest were primarily raised in 'humanistic,' liberal, middle-class families [Mankoff & Flacks, 1971, p. 54].

The same point was made in another way by Keniston in a letter to *Science* about the possible use of the American College Entrance questionnaire on attitudes and background for screening out potentially dissident students.

> There have already been dozens of empirical studies of students activists and protesters. Any college administrator with the diligence to read these studies already knows how to "screen out" the applicants who are most likely to engage in protest. As a start I would recommend that he admit only dull, unimaginative, conventional, and extremely devout applicants from conservative and politically apathetic families [Keniston, 1969, p. 1207].[1]

[1] Reprinted with permission from K. Keniston, ACE study of campus unrest. *Science,* 1969, *165,* 1206-1207. Copyright 1969 by the American Association for the Advancement of Science.

Family Background: Columbia College Panel Members

Given these statements by researchers in the field we expected a variety of measures of socioeconomic status to correlate positively with what we have called the protester's (attitude) profile. Therefore, the results relating to father's education that are presented in Table 5.1 were a surprise.

Not only were there no significant differences on any of the scales among sons of parents with different degrees of education, the slight deviations from the profile made no consistent sense. Although it was in accord with previous research to find the handful of students (13) whose fathers had less than a high school education to be highest on Traditional Moralism, it was hard to advance any plausible explanation for the lowest scores on the scale being sons of those with some college education, rather than of college graduates or those with professional training. It was also puzzling why sons of those with education beyond college should be lower on Machiavellian Cynicism and why sons of college graduates should be the lowest on Revolutionary Tactics, when both these scores correlate positively with radicalism. In short, students' New Left scale scores, which were generally very sensitive to involvement in protest, showed no significant relationship to fathers' education. The one aggregate that is closest to the "protesters' profile," sons of those with some college education, is precisely in the middle of the parental educational categories.

This finding of no relationship between student protest ideology and measures of parental status was puzzling. Why did we fail to find a relationship when almost all investigators had reported one? Our instruments should have been adequate to pick up such a relationship since we had already found that they afforded sharp discriminations between activists and nonactivists. Perhaps it was because the parents of Columbia students had higher socioeconomic status than would be true of most student samples. However, the same would be true of Flacks's (1967) sample at the University of Chicago, where the relationship between student dissent and parental status was evidently quite strong.

Family Background: Other College Samples

In examining various possibilities, we looked at the relationship between parental background and scale scores among members of the Columbia psychology class sample. Again, no relationship was found. At Columbia, at least, the failure to find the relationship was not a peculiarity of the members of the class of 1972 who were sampled. Similarly, the relationship between parental socioeconomic status and respondents' scale scores was examined in the New York University psychology class sample. Again, no relationship was found. Although

Table 5.1
Mean New Left Scale Scores of Columbia Panel Freshmen by Educational Level of Fathers

	N	Traditional Moralism	Machiavellian Tactics	Machiavellian Cynicism	New Left Philosophy	Revolutionary Tactics
Did not graduate high school	13	3.15	3.88	3.93	3.96	2.67
Graduated high school	17	2.96	3.49	3.79	3.76	3.01
Some college	20	2.58	3.38	3.93	3.97	2.83
Graduated college	21	2.95	3.77	4.07	3.42	2.47
Some graduate education	51	2.86	3.23	3.42	3.60	2.63

the coeducational New York University sample came from a more diverse and less privileged socioeconomic background than the Columbia samples, as a private school, New York University drew students from families who were able to pay a higher tuition than that required in public universities. This chain of reasoning led us to examine the relationship in community college samples. There again we found no differences.

Perhaps, we argued, the five failures to replicate the common finding that more highly educated parents had more radical progeny could be due to the fact that the parents of Columbia and New York University students had educational levels skewed toward the high end of a distribution of education of college parents in general, and the parents of community college students had educational levels that were skewed toward the lower end. Perhaps the relationship would appear in a sample of students whose parents varied more widely in educational attainment. The colleges to which we had access were characterized by admission policies that led to the selection of a preponderance of students from families who were different, although homogeneous, as far as parental status was concerned. One way of bypassing this selection problem would be to examine the relationship between parental education and student dissent in a precollege sample. However, this might introduce problems, because high schools in wealthy suburbs have students from better-educated families destined for more elite colleges compared to those in less affluent areas. This made it important to select a high school in a community with a varied population.

Family Background: A High School Sample

Our criteria for a high school sample were simple: (1) the students should come from a heterogeneous social base and (2) they should be available for testing. Because of prior hassles with school administrators, we bypassed official channels and obtained respondents on an informal basis. This introduced practical considerations; in using a "noncaptive audience" we had to reduce the number of questions asked in order to ensure cooperation. Therefore, the results are based on the summed total of 30 items selected from the 60 items of the revised form of the original New Left scale. Level of parental education was used as the background indicator. As can be seen in Table 5.2 there is a wide range of both fathers' and mothers' education. However, there is no relationship between either of these two variables and the children's New Left ideology scores.

By this time, our repeated failure to find the expected relationship between indicators of family status and student radicalism was intriguing. Perhaps there was something unique about New York City and its environs that was so conducive to radicalism that it washed out the relationship found previously in schools west of the Hudson and south of Long Island.

Table 5.2
Mean Abbreviated New Left Scale Scores of High School Students
by Educational Level of Mother and Father[a]

	Did not graduate high school	Graduated high school	Some college	College degree or more
Mother	3.47	3.29	3.54	3.50
	(*N*=24)	(*N*=95)	(*N*=32)	(*N*=37)
Father	3.53	3.30	3.35	3.49
	(*N*=24)	(*N*=49)	(*N*=36)	(*N*=77)

[a]All results based on abbreviated (30-item) version of the revised
New Left scale.

Family Background: A National Sample of College Students

One of the studies that had supported the previous findings that college
students who came from middle-class backgrounds were more liberal, if not
radical, in their ideology was conducted by the Danial Yankelovich research firm
in the early fall of 1968 for *Fortune* magazine (Yankelovich, 1969). Students in
a stratified sample of colleges were asked to choose between one of the
following statements:

> For me college is mainly a practical matter. With a college education I can earn
> more money, have a more interesting career, and enjoy a better position in society.

> I'm not really concerned with the practical benefits of college. I suppose that I
> take them for granted. College for me is something more intangible, perhaps the
> opportunity to change things rather than make out within the existing system.

The 54% of the students choosing the first alternative were dubbed career-
oriented and in the fall of 1968 tended to be more supportive of the Vietnam
War, more anti-civil liberties, and invariably more conservative on all issues than
their less career-oriented peers.

Those who chose the second alternative are of particular interest, since
they were more leftist on a variety of questions. At the beginning of the
1968-1969 school year, this group was characterized by coming from families
with higher occupational status and incomes—in fact, they were dubbed "post-
affluents." In the spring of 1969 Yankelovich did a second study of college
students, this time under the sponsorship of CBS. The relationship between
measures of parental status and career orientation of students did not appear as
it had in the study done 6 months earlier. In the report to CBS this failure to
find a relationship is indicated by Yankelovich's dropping the term "post-afflu-

ent" to describe non-career-oriented respondents. The term "forerunner" was used in its place, a term that did not suggest differences in socioeconomic status between the groups, but merely differences in ideology. (Presumably Yankelovich meant "forerunner" to be a truncated version of something like "forerunner of a new society.")

Questions of terminology aside, there are reasons for carefully examining the Yankelovich data. The first is that a fairly sophisticated question of political orientation was related to family status in September 1968 but not in March 1969. One might argue that the samples are differentially biased, but since the sampling procedures were similar, the biases should be constant and not affect the comparisons.

More crucial for our present concern, however, is Yankelovich's use of 15 of our items in the 1969 CBS survey (see Appendix B-3). Scores on this index of radicalism were compared with students' reports of parental occupation and income. (Education of parents was not ascertained in the survey.) Fathers' occupation was coded using the Hollingshead index. We found no significant relationship between occupational status and the scores on the index of radicalism. A comparison of reported family income and index scores similarly yielded no relationship.

Our findings were consistent. No matter what measure of protest ideology we used—the 60-item New Left scale profile in its original form or in the more simply worded revised form, the 30 items comprising an abbreviated New Left scale, or the 15-item index used in the Yankelovich-CBS national sample—the results were the same. There was no significant relationship between any of these measures of endorsement of protest ideology and available indicators of parental socioeconomic level, whether the indicator be education, occupation, or income. This was true for student samples from Columbia College, other New York colleges, and a Long Island high school, as well as for a nationwide sample of students.

If the relationship existed at the time we did our studies, it was so elusive that none of our measures detected it. Before discussing possible reasons for not finding such a relationship, let us examine two other background factors sometimes posited as relating to student protest: religion and ancestral origin.

Parents' Religion

An examination of parents' religious preferences and students' scores on the five New Left scales was conducted for six samples where the question was asked. The respondents were divided into four groups—Protestant, Catholic, Jewish, and those indicating no church membership—based on the religious preference of their mothers and of their fathers.

In none of the samples was parents' religious preference, whether Protestant, Catholic, Jewish, or "none," significantly related to the respondents' scores on Revolutionary Tactics. In only one instance was there a difference on New Left Philosophy—this occurred among students at Corning Community College, where children of Protestant mothers and those whose mothers had no religion scored higher than children of Catholic mothers. There was only one respondent with Jewish parents in this sample. The relationship did not hold, however, for fathers' religious preference among the same group of respondents. In two schools, New York University and Fordham School of Social Work, a relationship was found between Traditional Moralism scores and both parents' religious preference. Students with Catholic parents scored highest, those describing their parents' religion as "none" scored lowest, and those with Jewish or Protestant parents scored in-between. The same trend appeared in the Columbia College sample but was not significant.

A more detailed examination of parental religion was made on the New York University sample, where respondents were asked to be specific about their parents' religion. In a breakdown of Jewish parents (Orthodox, Conservative, Reform) no significant pattern of relationships emerged. A breakdown of Protestant sects into fundamentalist (Baptist, Lutheran, etc.) and liberal (Unitarian, Presbyterian, etc.) also did not indicate any differences.

In sum, the only consistent pattern was a slight relationship between scores on Traditional Moralism and parental religion. When the data reach significance, it is attributable to differences between respondents with Catholic parents and those whose parents have no religious affiliation.

Ancestral Origin

Part of common folklore, especially among some conservatives, is that protest is alien to American values and indicates "foreign" influences. There is some evidence supporting this belief. Flacks in his study of Chicago area students in 1965 and 1966 noted that, "the great majority of activists' grandparents were foreign born [Flacks, 1967, p. 65]." Braungart (1971) reports on a 1966-1967 sample of over 1200 college students derived from 10 eastern colleges and universities and from two national samples of SDS and YAF members. After a methodologically sophisticated multivariate analysis of background characteristics of the students in his samples, he notes that leftist student activists are drawn from southern or eastern European backgrounds, while right-wing youth come from higher-status northern European backgrounds.

The participants in four of our samples were asked to indicate how many of their grandparents were born in the United States. We found no relationship between the number of grandparents born abroad and their grandchildren's scores on any of the five scales among members of the Columbia psychology class or at Corning Community College. Those in the New York University psychology class who had one or more grandparents born abroad scored slightly but significantly higher on Traditional Moralism than those who were at least third-generation Americans. This, of course, is a trend in the opposite direction from what would be predicted given the protesters' profile. Similarly, at Suffolk Community College those whose grandparents were native born scored higher on New Left Philosophy than did those who had one or more grandparents born abroad.

There is, thus, little evidence from the respondents in these samples who took the scales during the 1968-1969 school year that there is any substantial relationship between grandparents' national origin and student ideology. If anything, the relationship is the reverse of what has been previously reported.

On Resolving Discrepant Findings:
The 1968-1969 Watershed Phenomenon

Our failure to find relationships between family status and student protest had, as mentioned earlier, puzzled us. Being reasonably careful, if not picayune, about the collection and analysis of our data, we were confident of our findings. But why were they out of step with the conclusions drawn by equally conscientious researchers?

At the time we started our investigations in 1968, all published and unpublished research with which we were familiar had been conducted before the wave of student protests began. With the exception of a study by Somers (1965) at Berkeley during the free speech crisis, all of these had reported a positive relationship between indicators of familial status and protest proneness. The Yankelovich-CBS survey in the early fall of 1968 reported the same finding; the one conducted the following spring did not. Gradually other material accumulated supporting our belief that by 1969 there was no longer a significant relationship between parental status and student New Left protest. Two national surveys on samples of college students in 1970 and 1971 yielded no relationship (Yankelovich, 1972). A study by Gergen and Gergen (1970) on a sample of over 2000 students in a variety of American colleges in 1969-1970 similarly showed no relationship.

Our argument, then, is that the differences between pre-1968 findings and our post-1968 results are not artifactual. We suggest that when the protest movement was relatively small and a minority of students were involved, a relationship between family background and radical political activity existed. But once the movement spread and large numbers of students were involved, the protesters included students from a variety of demographic, religious, and ethnic backgrounds, and hence the previous relationship tended to disappear. This explanation is similar to one independently advanced by Mankoff and Flacks (1971) from their analysis of data from the University of Wisconsin, a school with an early history of radicalization. In the spring of 1968 they questioned a sample of students who had signed a petition protesting the disciplining of some of their peers for participation in a demonstration against Dow Chemical in November 1967. Mankoff and Flacks found that those students who had participated in protest activities for a period of 3 years prior to the demonstration, that is, "veteran cadre," did indeed come from families that were disproportionately urban, Jewish, and well-educated as compared to nonsigners. But for the students who were latecomers to radicalism the relationship was barely visible (and nonsignificant).

It seems, then, that 1968-1969 was a watershed year for studies dealing with family status and student radicalism. Most if not all of the research on student protest that was done during or prior to that year found positive relationships between family status and student protest; most if not all of the research done since 1968-1969 has found no such relationship.

Dissecting the Generation Gap

The lack of relationship between measures of family status and protest proneness on the part of students had an unanticipated consequence. It made us think seriously about some of the assumptions underlying differences and similarities between generations and about ways of testing them.

One obvious way of studying generational differences is to apply relevant questionnaires and scales to members of the parent generation and to those of the children's generation. Mean differences on the measures between the older and younger generation would indicate the extent to which they were similar or the extent to which the younger had drifted away from the values of the older generation. This is essentially the logic of surveys from representative samples in which the age cohort of the parents' generation are compared with those of younger respondents. Such studies, however, assume that the differences in values between a random sample of adults in the age cohort of the parents' population and that of a random group of those in the age cohort of the children's generation would be identical to differences found between samples of parents and their own children. In fact, direct comparisons on relevant measures between young adults and their own parents are extremely rare.

Such mean comparisons of differences, whether made by comparing relevant age cohorts or matched parent-child samples, do not yield information about the dynamics of change. To obtain this we also need to examine intrafamilial differences, that is, the correlation between the scores of a particular parent and those of his/her own child. If scores are in the same relative position within the two samples (positive correlations), this would indicate that the two generations have "convergent" values; to the extent that they differed (zero or negative correlations), the data would indicate divergence between the two generations.

It is possible to compare mean differences and correlations on any two samples for which parallel data are collected. This produces interesting possibilities for analysis when one sample is composed of parents and the other is composed of their children. We shall provide a few hypothetical models to illustrate different interpretations of patterns of similarity and difference in generational comparisons. We shall use the term *drift* to indicate mean differences between the two samples; the higher the mean difference the higher the drift. We shall use the term *divergence* to indicate differences in the correlation between parents and children; the further the correlation from the upper limit of + 1.00, the greater the divergence.

"IDEAL MODELS" OF INTERGENERATIONAL COMPARISON

No Drift/No Divergence. The simplest situation of all would be one in which there were no ideological drift from one generation to the next and in which every conservative parent begat a young Tory and every restive parent produced a young radical. This relationship is plotted in Figure 5.1. It will be noted that we are assuming in the figure that parents and children are being measured on the same scale, that higher numerical scores indicate higher radicalism, and that there is roughly normal distribution of scores on the part of both generations. The vertical lines connecting points on the two horizontal scales connect a parent and his/her scale value with that of his/her progeny. We are not in a position to know whether any known society ever approximated such a model, but it illustrates an idealized version of the transmission of values from generation to generation in what might be described as traditional societies.

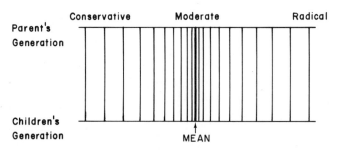

Figure 5.1. "No drift/no divergence."

High Drift/No Divergence. In this model it is assumed that the younger generation is more radical than the generation of its parents (it could be more
conservative, but this condition does not seem to have been so common in
contemporary Western society), but that parents and children occupy the same
relative position within their respective ranges of scores (see Figure 5.2). If such
a pattern were found, it would suggest that broad social factors unrelated to
family dynamics were having a pervasive effect upon the younger generation. It
is difficult to conceive of an actual situation in which such broad social tides
would not have some disruptive effects upon parent-child relationships, but we
are concerned here only with the implications of a hypothetical model.

No Drift/High Divergence. This hypothetical model would show that crucial
factor affecting intergenerational differences as being the rebellion of the young
within families. In its extreme form this would result in the most reactionary
parents having the most radical progeny and the most radical parents having
ultraconservative offspring. The plotted model is shown in Figure 5.3. Again, it
is difficult to imagine an intergenerational game of ideological musical chairs of
this sort actually occurring. This is merely a schematic representation of comparisons in which there is no mean change and a correlation approaching the
limit of -1.00.

High Drift/High Divergence. The final logical combination of extreme measures
would imply not only that the younger generation was in rebellion, but that
pervasive charges were taking place within the society, causing children to drift
from their parents' values (see Figure 5.4).

Regression toward the Mean: No Drift/Moderate Divergence. In contrast to the
above idealized models, what should we expect if an analysis of the data revealed
a classic regression toward the mean? Parents would then be serving neither as
models (characterized by low divergence, i.e., high positive correlations) nor as
targets for rebellion (high divergence, i.e., high negative correlations). Let us
further assume that no major social changes were occurring and that there was

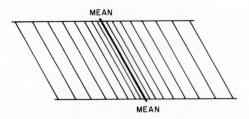

Figure 5.2. "High drift/no divergence."

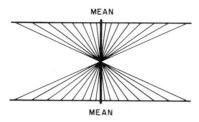

Figure 5.3. "No drift/high divergence."

thus no mean difference (i.e., no drift). This situation is plotted in Figure 5.5. Hypothetically, if parents had an infinite number of children and regression was operating, the distribution of the reactionaries' sons' scores would have a mean in the conservative area (halfway between the mean of their parents and that of the entire parents' generation), the distribution of the moderates' children would have a mean similar to that of their parents, and the radicals' children would have a mean halfway between that of their parents and that of the parents' population. Here we would expect a moderate positive correlation because high-scoring parents would have moderately high-scoring sons and low-scoring parents would have moderately low-scoring sons. This would imply a familial transmission of values contaminated by measurement error.

A DIRECT COMPARISON BETWEEN PARENTS AND SONS

As indicated in Chapter 3, we collected data on the parents of members of the Columbia panel sample in the summer of 1970 by mailing copies of questionnaires to the parents of those sons who had remained in school and did not object to their parents filling out the questionnaires. The only significant difference between those returning questionnaires and those not replying was that a greater proportion of the sons of returnees reported their parents as engaging in political activity than did the sons of the nonreturnees.

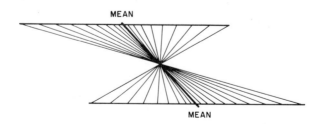

Figure 5.4. "High drift/high divergence."

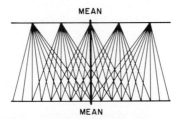

Figure 5.5. Diagram of "regression toward the mean, no drift/moderate divergence."

In order to test the fit of the hypothetical models presented in the preceding section to our data, two analyses were performed: Mean scores on the same scales were compared for parents and children to determine drift, and the correlations between the scores of parents and children were computed to determine divergence and regression. The results of the two analyses will be discussed separately.

The mean scores for the parents and sons on all five scales are presented in Table 5.3. There are several points of interest about these differences in scores. With the exception of scores on Machiavellian Tactics, there are no differences between mothers' and fathers' mean scores. The fathers' higher scores on Machiavellian Tactics as compared to mothers' scores are consistent with material on sex differences among college students (Christie 1970b), and the lack of mother-father differences on the other four scales also parallels our failure to find consistent sex differences in college samples (see Chapter 6). Intergenerational drift is found on almost all scales, and in each case suggests that sons are more radical than their parents. The sons have significantly lower scores on

Table 5.3
Means and Standard Deviations for Parents and Their Sons (Panel Sample) on the Five New Left Scales[a]

	N	Traditional Moralism		Machiavellian Tactics		Machiavellian Cynicism		New Left Philosophy		Revolutionary Tactics	
		X	SD	X	SD	X	SD	X	SD	X	SD
Mothers	90	3.53	.88	3.04	.73	3.21	.67	3.51	.76	2.02	.63
Sons	90	2.72	.87	3.32	.71	3.88	.79	3.83	1.10	3.13	1.13
Fathers	75	3.55	.98	3.43	.70	3.09	.62	3.38	.90	2.02	.63
Sons	75	2.67	.73	3.24	.72	3.86	.77	3.83	1.08	3.16	1.09

[a]Data on parents gathered during summer of 1970; data on sons gathered in fall of 1969.

Traditional Moralism. On Machiavellian Cynicism and on Revolutionary Tactics, the sons score significantly higher. The sons' scores on New Left Philosophy are also significantly higher but not as markedly so. The only scale on which the sons' scores do not differ from those of their parents in the direction of the protester's profile is on Machiavellian Tactics, where they have slightly lower scores than their fathers and significantly higher ones than their mothers.

We next examined the data for evidence of divergence. The patterns of correlation are presented in Table 5.4. The correlation between fathers' and mothers' scores on every scale is significantly positive. We cannot determine the extent to which this is a true reflection of similar ideology or the result of possible parental collaboration. The scales were sent out by mail and the instructions were to answer them independently. There is indirect evidence that these were adhered to, at least partially, since the parents' respective mean scores on Machiavellian Tactics do differ significantly in the same direction as that found in previous research.

More relevant to the question of divergence, however, is the fact that in every instance the correlation between parent and son is lower than between father and mother. The magnitude of the parent-son correlations is in general low, although 2 of the 10 are significant at the .01 level and two are significant at the .05 level of confidence. The scale with the highest correlations between sons and parents is Traditional Moralism (mother-son $r = .32$, father-son $r = .31$). This is, of course, the scale that, as its title implies, taps long enduring values, and it is the one which would be most closely tied to familial experiences. The scale with the lowest correlations is Revolutionary Tactics (mother-son $r = .08$, father-son $r = .04$). The items on this scale were couched in the rhetoric of student radicalism, and the values expressed were probably not ones the students learned from their parents.

Overall then, it appears that there is a marked intergenerational drift toward radicalism, but that the measures of intergenerational divergence generally supported neither convergence with nor rebellion from parents' ideology.

A CLOSER LOOK AT GENERATIONAL DIFFERENCES IN
REVOLUTIONARY TACTICS

There is no major interpretative problem in grasping the meaning of a high positive or negative correlation. An experienced investigator can visualize the scatter plot. An essentially zero-order correlation, however can mask a variety of relationships that exist in the data. The correlation of + .04 between fathers' and sons' scores on Revolutionary Tactics may reflect a pattern of true randomness between the values of the two generations, but on the other hand it might conceal countervailing trends. With this possibility in mind we were particularly

Table 5.4

Correlations between Scores of Mothers, Fathers, and Sons (Panel Sample) on the Five New Left Scales[a]

	N	Traditional Moralism	Machiavellian Tactics	Machiavellian Cynicism	New Left Philosophy	Revolutionary Tactics
Mother with father	72	$.53^b$	$.51^b$	$.39^b$	$.56^b$	$.55^b$
Mother with son	90	$.32^b$	.16	.15	$.22^b$	.08
Father with son	75	$.31^b$	$.25^b$	.04	.18	.04

[a]Data on parents gathered during summer of 1970; data on sons gathered fall of 1969.
[b]$p<.05$, correlation greater than zero.

interested in more closely examining the scatter plot between fathers' and sons' scores.

Revolutionary Tactics was of greatest interest among the five scales because:

1. It discriminated the most sharply between student activists and nonactivists.
2. It discriminated most sharply between extremist political groups.
3. It discriminated most sharply between parents and sons.

We selected the father-son comparison because of its relevance to Freudian-tinged notions about the rebellion of sons against fathers. But the following results are applicable to the comparison of mothers' and sons' scores as well.

We have plotted the scores of father and sons in Figure 5.6 following the procedure described earlier to indicate different models of drift and discrepancy between generations. Every father's score is indicated along the upper horizontal line; every son's score is indicated along the lower horizontal line. A light line connects every father's and every son's score. A heavy diagonal line connects the means of the two distributions; two moderately heavy lines connected the points that are one standard deviation above and below the means of the respective distributions.

It can be seen that the resulting figure conforms to none of the idealized models suggested earlier. The marked intergenerational drift noted in the preceding section is clearly apparent. There is not enough crossover of scores for a pure discrepancy model, yet the pattern of extremist fathers having more moderate sons seems to go beyond what one would expect from regression toward the mean. The correlation of +.04 falls much lower than the expected one of +.50 which would be true if regression toward the mean were the only factor operating, and the pattern of connections does not seem to be purely random, as the correlation of +.04 suggests.

In examining the distribution in more detail, we divided the fathers into four

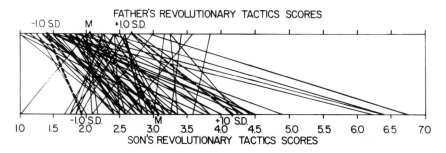

Figure 5.6. Comparison of fathers' and sons' scores on the Revolutionary Tactics scale (Columbia panel sample).

groups: those scoring more than one standard deviation below the mean, those scoring less than one standard deviation below the mean, those scoring less than one standard deviation above the mean, and those scoring more than one standard deviation above the mean. We then computed the means for the four groups and the expected means of their sons' scores if there was regression toward the mean. These relationships are plotted in Figure 5.7. Although the pattern does look similar to that expected by a regression model, the mean scores of the sons (adjusted for drift) regress further toward the mean of the fathers' distribution than can be accounted for by simple regression. By chance we would expect that one-half of the sons would fall short of the predicted regression line and one-half of them would fall beyond it. Actually, only 23 sons' scores fall short and 52 fall beyond the regression line. This difference from the chance value of .5 is significant by a binomial test at the .05 level.

With this sample of fathers and sons, the most sensitive scale we have of students radicalism indicates that a simple inheritance model of political ideology is not applicable. The most radical and most conservative fathers tended to have moderate sons, and most of the extremist sons had moderate fathers. However, the significant tendency for sons' scores to deviate more than expected by simple regression is not sufficient to support a model of strong rebellion against the father's position; none of the conservative fathers had a radical son, and only one radical father had a conservative son. Rather, our results suggest

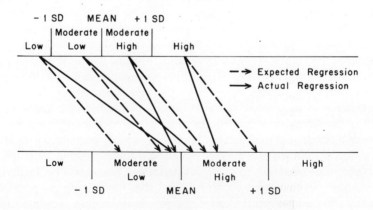

Figure 5.7. Expected and actual regression from fathers' grouped means to sons' mean score on the Revolutionary Tactics scale (Columbia panel sample).

that a cross between two of the models, high drift/high divergence and regression toward the mean, best describes the data.

To the best of our knowledge no one has reported an analysis in which the relationships between parents' and children's scores were analyzed using scatter plots in this fashion. Connell (1972), in a review of all known studies conducted prior to 1968 in which parents' scores on political measures were compared with those of their children, reported that the correlations were generally low, a finding in accord with our data. Since more detailed analyses of the patterns of relationship were not made, we do not know whether analyses similar to our own would yield comparable results or whether our findings reflect a unique set of relationships.

AN INTERGENERATIONAL IMPULSE TO ACTIVISM?

The findings presented thus far suggest that parents' attitudes had little effect on their sons' political stance. But before concluding the chapter let us present some additional data that may help clarify this relationship between the generations. At the time the sophomore questionnaire was given, the members of the Columbia panel sample were asked to describe their parents' political activities. It was possible to code the responses according to whether the parents were politically active or inactive and according to nature of the activities. In Table 5.5 the extent of parents' political activity is compared with sons' political activity, categorized as described in Chapter 4.

Politically active parents appear more likely to have sons who are dissident activists than do politically quiescent parents. The chi-square of 15.15 is significant beyond the .01 level. This relationship holds regardless of the ideological bent of the parents' activity. Sons of parents who had worked for the Socialist party during the 1930s are just as likely to have engaged in confrontation-type activities before college as are sons of parents who had run for town mayor.

These data are especially interesting when compared with data from a study by Thomas (1971), completed just prior to the wave of protests in 1968. He found that children of both conservative and liberal politically active parents participated in conventional politics to the same degree as the 10% most politically active adults in the United States. But at that time it was only the children of liberal parents who participated in protest activities, a finding congruent with the other pre-1968 research on student protesters. Braungart (1971), also using information gathered prior to 1968, found that family political position and argumentation (about politics) were the two variables that accounted for the most variance in a path analysis of student protest activity. If argumentation can be construed as a reflection of political activism, as seems plausible, his results may well be in line with those bits of evidence that point to the importance of parental political concern and activity per se, rather than the variety of ideologi-

Table 5.5
Relationship between Reported Political Involvement of Parents
and Sons (Panel Sample)

Parents	Sons			
	Nonactivist	Sympathizer	Dissident activist	Total
Politically active	13	13	28	54
Politically inactive	34	20	13	67
Totals	47	33	41	121

cal content, in predicting children's political behavior. It is also likely that such parental concern is a predictor insensitive to changes in the social context of the New Left movement, such as those changes that occurred between 1968 and 1969 and that appear to have led to a lessening of the relationship between student protest and parental demographic variables.

Summary

Failure to find any relationship in our samples between family status and students' protest ideology led to a reexamination of other studies. It appears that higher-status families did produce a slightly higher proportion of dissidents in the earlier stages of the New Left movement. After the spread of student protests in 1968-1969 and the involvement of large number of students, the base of protest became so broad that the earlier relationship disappeared.

The magnitude of the correlations between attitudes of mothers and sons and fathers and sons varied with the nature of the attitude measured. Correlations on the Traditional Moralism scale were the highest of the five scales; those on Revolutionary Tactics were the lowest. In addition, sons were significantly more radical than their parents on four of the five scales. An interesting finding of unknown generalizability was that fathers with more extreme ideologies (be they left or right) tended to have relatively moderate sons, and that extremist (right or left) sons tended to have relatively moderate fathers.

It was concluded on the basis of studies to date that familial background variables, with the possible exception of parental political activism, contributed relatively little to student activism after 1968-1969.

6

Academic and Demographic Variables Relating to Protest Ideology

Since there was no support for the expected correlation between the ideology of parents and that of their sons nor between the socioeconomic status of parents and the ideology of their sons, we explored other possible correlates of radicalism. In this chapter, we report analyses of data relevant to some stereotypes of radical students.

Academic Variables

First, we examined variables associated with a student's academic role. Our reading of both New Left publications and professional journals suggested that campus protesters might be more antiscience, more intelligent, less vocationally oriented, and less likely to stay in school than their conservative peers (Finney, 1971; Lewis & Kraut, 1972).

ANTISCIENCE ATTITUDES

In recent years, dissident students have at times been portrayed as opposed to scientific and social scientific research. Ironically, this was a position traditionally held by conservative students, resisting invasions of personal privacy. Although our impressions, based on informal contacts with undergraduates, did not support the idea that radicals were antiscience, we decided to investigate the issue. We knew from responses to the New Left scale that radicals believed that research that might be used "contrary to the social good" should not be supported (see Table 2.5). Our interest was in whether such a belief led to a principled rejection of social scientific research regardless of its nature.

The first test of this proposition was based on data collected from the 153-member Columbia sample. When participants completed questionnaires during the fall of their freshman year, they were told of the possibility of a follow-up study and asked to indicate their willingness to participate in it. A comparison of attitudes from the five scales was made between those who at the time were willing to continue and those who were not. The direction of the differences on all measures, although insignificant, suggested a relationship the reverse of what might have been anticipated—those who wanted to participate were more radical than those who did not. There was also no apparent curvilinear relationship, which would be expected if both radicals and conservatives had an antiscientific bias.

Members of a graduate research seminar designed an experiment to explore the question more rigorously. The study measured how quickly students differing in New Left orientations aborted a psychological experiment in which it became increasingly apparent that the study had implications of social repressiveness. Potential subjects were chosen from a pool of Columbia students who had taken the introductory psychology course the preceding year; almost all had taken the revised version of the New Left scale. Students who had not taken subsequent courses in psychology were telephoned on a random basis by a female graduate student; she gave her name, said she was a student in a social psychology course, and inquired if the person called had taken introductory psychology the previous year. She then asked the person to participate in an experiment. She persisted until a definite appointment was made or until there was a refusal. No mention was made of a sponsorship or of what the experiment was about.

The experiment itself was designed to involve the participant in research with onerous social implications. When the participant arrived he was greeted by the young woman who had called him and introduced to the student who was conducting the experiment. The experimenter gave the participant a four-page explanation of the study which discussed the use of the galvanic skin response in lie detector tests. It included reference to actual studies and to studies done by the "investigative team" sponsoring the present research. These later reports were in fact fabrications. It was argued:

> One of the reasons lie detection tests are fallible is that many of the "neutral" words used as filler items are based on lists that are out of date and that many of the words are not "neutral" for most subjects so that false positive responses are elicited in many cases. We, on the other hand, have through research, developed a list of words which are empirically neutral for contemporary samples. Our other improvement is to draw upon the work of Orne and Rosenthal on experimenter bias. Since in usual lie detection procedure the interrogator knows which words are related to the crime, he frequently stresses the critical words or otherwise consciously or

unconsciously pronounces them differently than would someone naive to the crime and the alleged suspect.

The subject was then told that he would be the experimenter. He thus found himself in the position of being an interrogator in a lie detection study.

The "suspect" (actually a confederate, who was introduced as a student from General Studies) was then brought in and introduced as one who had committed an "experimental" crime. The suspect was then seated, the experimenter attached electrodes to his wrists, and there was a 5-minute period in which the suspect sat quietly in order to obtain a steady base rate. During this period the subject read the list of stimulus words to be used. He was asked to check off on a separate sheet, any of the words, that he thought might be relevant to the "crime." He was also asked to check any words that seemed unusual for a lie detection test. None of the subjects indicated any suspicion of the words or the test at this point.

The subject was then asked to read a list of stimulus words to the suspect, and as he did so it became increasingly evident that the subject was becoming resistant. The stooge initially gave political responses to stimulus words that were superficially innocuous: "band" in response to "arm," "gas" to "tier," "Engels" to "marks," etc. After first noting and then protesting the political nature of the stimulus words, the suspect tried to persuade the interrogator to make a deal to fake the data. Then he accused the interrogator of working for the CIA, and finally he refused to respond. This sequence of responses had been deliberately designed to make aborting the experiment progressively more consistent with the ideology of student radicals.

The experiment permitted several different stages at which to assess the antiscientific bias of the New Left. Those who were most opposed to research should have refused to participate when first called to the phone. Of the 27 students approached, the only 2 who would not participate were among the most radical. One was a clear case of a radical refusing because he did not believe in cooperating with any Establishment research. The other refusal was by a very active member of the Progressive Labor Party. He pleaded lack of time because he was preparing for a hearing on his activities during an antirecruiting demonstration on campus. He did, however, promise to participate once his hearing was over and volunteered the names of several friends who he believed would be interested. At first we considered the possibility that this rebel was really antiresearch but too gallant to reject flatly the entreaties of a persuasive female. However, a check of the records revealed that he had actually participated as a subject in six psychology experiments during the previous term, twice as many as required.

The next stage at which we expected dropouts was following the experimental instructions, in which it was pointed out that the "improved" lie detection procedure to be used had practical implications; the research was designed to produce a technique that could be used by nonprofessional personnel for the efficient detection of guilt. Only one participant refused to start the experiment after receiving these instructions. His argument was that the technique would be used on students and blacks, not on professors or other members of the Establishment. He was very active in protest politics and had, the year before, not turned in his answer sheet to the New Left scale because he did not believe in providing authorities with any measure of student ideology.

Eleven other students refused to continue their participation at various points during the experiment proper. A comparison of the New Left scale scores of those continuing to the end with those who did not revealed a slight but insignificant tendency for the more radical students to abort earlier. Neither during the experiment nor during the course of a lengthy debriefing was there indication that participants doubted the scientific legitimacy of the study or its possible usefulness to law enforcement agencies.

The failure of significant numbers of students purporting radical beliefs to refuse to participate or to abort the experiment seems to indicate that there is not a great deal of antiscience bias among this particular group of left-wing college students. This finding, however, does not preclude the possibility that such a sentiment may be found among a more radical population, as suggested by the flat refusal by one of the most radical of those contacted before having any knowledge of the nature of the experiment. A similar refusal was encountered from the most left-wing respondent in the basic 153-member Columbia sample when he was asked to be interviewed during the spring of his freshman year. He was the only one of the 53 students approached at that time who would not participate.

MEASURES OF ACADEMIC ABILITIES

SAT Scores. Contrary to expectations, there were no significant correlations for the 153 Columbia freshmen in the basic sample between their SAT scores and their scores on any of the five New Left scales. This was true whether the verbal and quantitative scores were examined separately or in combination. It could be argued that the lack of a relationship results from the restricted distribution of SATs among those accepted to Columbia College. Since the range was from 445 to 800 and the standard deviation for this sample on the verbal and quantitative tests was 77.3 and 65.5, respectively, this explanation does not seem plausible. Given the high reliability of the scores, such a range should have provided indications of a relationship, had one existed.

One further possibility occurred to us. Although verbal and quantitative scores are, in general, highly correlated with one another, some students tend to score relatively high on the verbal scale, compared to the quantitative, and others show the opposite pattern. The first is sometimes referred to as the "poet's profile" and the second as the "engineer's profile." Since faculty and students in the humanities and social sciences are more likely to be politically radical whereas those in applied fields tend to be politically quiescent (Lipset & Ladd, 1970), we examined the SAT discrepancy scores among our sample members. Again no significant findings emerged. We were, however, somewhat thwarted by admissions standards. Relatively few applicants with high discrepancy scores had been admitted.

Grades. Respondents in two samples, the Columbia introductory psychology class and New York University introductory psychology class, were asked to indicate their overall grade-point average. These reports were then compared to scores on the five basic scales. No significant differences emerged; radical students were no more or less likely to report receiving good grades than their more conservative peers.

Relevant to an interpretation of these findings is the brief period on which grades were based. While most of the students in the Columbia sample were in the spring of their second year of college they had only two terms of grades behind them because of pass-fail options issued during the semester of the campus disruptions. Over one-half of the New York University sample were freshmen, and their average represented only one semester's work. The failure to find a relationship between attitudes and grades may, therefore, have been due to the instability of the grade-point average measure itself.

CAREER ORIENTATIONS

Educational Philosophy. Another variable we were concerned with was the educational philosophy of students. We asked respondents from the Columbia College psychology class sample and from New York University and Corning and Suffolk Community Colleges to choose between two statements representing different views toward a college education that had originally been used by Yankelovich in his cross-national student surveys (see Chapter 5). The first stresses the pragmatic aspects of college training for a future career. The second stresses a liberal arts philosophy of learning for its own sake. The data are presented in Table 6.1.

In all samples, students choosing the career-oriented alternative score significantly higher on Traditional Moralism ($p < .05$). At Columbia and New York University, the pragmatic group presents a profile similar to that of the nonactivist students: low on New Left Philosophy, Revolutionary Tactics, and Machiavellian Cynicism, and high on Machiavellian Tactics and Traditional Moralism. The data from the Corning and Suffolk samples tend to follow a similar pattern.

Table 6.1
Comparison of New Left Scale Scores of Samples as a Function of Educational Philosophy

Sample	N	Traditional Moralism	Machiavellian Tactics	Machiavellian Cynicism	New Left Philosophy	Revolutionary Tactics
			Career Oriented			
Columbia (psychology class)	28	3.08[a]	3.89[a]	3.77[a]	3.49[a]	2.92[a]
New York University	110	3.17[a]	3.68[a]	4.16	3.74[a]	3.03[a]
Corning Community College	38	3.40[a]	3.56[a]	3.76	3.78	2.93
Suffolk Community College	45	3.51[a]	3.72	3.93[a]	3.68	2.80
			Learning for its own sake			
Columbia (psychology class)	75	2.11	3.13	4.30	4.40	3.80
New York University	91	2.57	3.17	4.37	4.30	3.34
Corning Community College	26	2.78	3.15	3.98	4.06	3.07
Suffolk Community College	18	2.92	3.57	4.76	3.94	2.93

[a] $p < .05$, t test between career-oriented and learning-for-its-own-sake groups within designated sample.

In the nationwide college study by Yankelovich, the question was asked of 747 respondents. The results were supportive. Those who primarily wanted to gain knowledge and insight at college scored significantly higher ($p<.01$) on a shortened version of the New Left scale.

We also looked at the correlation between the percentage of students at a particular school choosing the practical alternative and the degree of radicalism at that school. Whether radicalism is measured by New Left scale attitudes or by percentage of activists in the sample, its rank order with educational philosophy among the four schools is perfect. Columbia, the most radical, had only 25% who were career oriented; New York University had 55%, Corning had 60%, and finally, Suffolk, the least radical, had 71% of the sample looking for practical experience at college.

Choice of College Major. In the tradition of research on student samples, we asked the usual question about each respondent's actual or intended major field of concentration. Few consistent patterns emerged. Among the New York University sample those with intentions to major in the humanities and social sciences scored significantly lower on the Traditional Moralism and Machiavellian Tactics scales and higher on New Left Philosophy than those in the sciences and applied areas. Students at Suffolk who majored in liberal arts as opposed to business administration and other applied fields scored significantly lower on the Traditional Moralism scale. There were no differences on any of the scales for the Columbia University or Corning Community College students, the other samples of which this question was asked.

A probable reason for this lack of differentiation is that the data from these samples were collected early in the students' college career. Although orientations toward educational goals existed, the institutional implementation of these nascent orientations had not yet been translated into definite choices. Recent studies that have sampled large groups of upperclassmen and graduate students have found those majoring in the humanities and social science to be more radical than the rest of the student body (Auger, Barton, & Maurice, 1970; Geller & Howard, 1972; Kerpelman, 1972). Another possible contributing factor was the growing negative reaction toward college requirements among students, accompanied by a resistance to settling on a major field. By fall of their sophomore year 11% of the Columbia panel sample had not decided on a major and almost one-third had no idea of their career choice. The lack of specific plans for the future, highlighted in some of the interview quotations previously cited (Chapter 2), is also symptomatic of this trend.

ACADEMIC SURVIVAL

It had been informally noted by college administrators that the college dropout rate had increased during the late 1960s, despite the fact that continued enrollment provided protection against the draft for male students. Given the general anti-Establishment theme of the New Left scale, we might expect radicals to be more likely to drop out. In fact, as was noted earlier, the more rebellious college students had profiles similar to college dropouts who were self-proclaimed revolutionaries.

At the end of their junior year, the spring of 1971, 113 students of the 153 in the freshman sample were still enrolled at Columbia College. We obtained material from the dean's office on the then current academic status of these respondents and compared freshman year scores of those still in school with those who had voluntarily left. This comparison is presented in Figure 6.1. The figure reveals no significant differences in scale scores between those still in school and those who dropped out.[1] Left-wing rebels were as likely to stay in school as their less revolutionary peers. However we cannot generalize from this sample to schools with different institutional policies regarding disruptive students; there has been a long history of supportive action for students at Columbia College. During the period the present sample was in school, student disrupters were more likely to be put on probation than expelled. The attrition in this group was therefore primarily determined by nonadministrative initiative. It should also be noted that the scores on which comparisons were made were administered early in the freshman year. It is therefore possible that the dropouts became radicalized while at Columbia, and hence left college. But it is our impression from our informal knowledge of the respondents that such an explanation does not account for the majority of those who were not registered at Columbia at the end of their junior year.

In sum, it would appear that the educational goals of radicals are more attuned to discovery and exploration of self and others, as contrasted to the more conventional and pragmatic goals of conservatives. Despite this more subjective approach to education, the two groups did not differ appreciably in ability, grades, or survival in an academic setting. Our evidence also indicates that while radicals generally were more concerned with the social implications of the use of scientific research, only some extreme radicals were totally antiscience. Thus, the popular picture of the radical as highly intellectual and ideologically opposed to science would not seem to be borne out by the data we have gathered. However, since most of the previous research on which this stereotype is based was done before the movement reached its peak, it is likely that by the time our data were gathered these characteristics no longer differentiated radical students from their more conservative peers. Such an interpretation would be consistent with the data presented in the previous chapter on the lack of relationship between parental background characteristics and the ideology of their children. The findings concerning the relationship between intelligence and activism are a

---

[1] A similar finding was reported in Chapter 3 for students who had left Columbia at the end of their freshman year, as compared with those who remained.

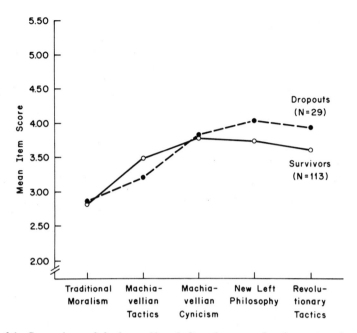

Figure 6.1. Comparison of freshman New Left scale scores for dropouts and survivors. (Does not include 10 students suspended or on leave of absence and 1 student deceased as of June 1971. Status was determined during spring semester of junior year.)

case in point. In 1965, Somers reported a positive correlation between the variables for Berkeley students. Kerpelman (1972) gathered data from three colleges during the 1968-1969 academic year and found no differences.

Demographic Variables

To complete the inventory of possible correlates of radicalism, we examined some basic sociological variables: sex, age, education level attained, and religion.

SEX

There were eight samples (Oregon State, Corning, Suffolk, Fordham, New York University, New York adults, parents, private school teachers) with enough male and female respondents to allow comparisons between sexes. Only one systematic difference across these samples emerged; males scored higher than females on the Machiavellian Tactics scale, a finding predicted by previous research (Christie 1970b). This pattern was exhibited in all samples and was significant in four of them.

While there were two other significant differences[2] among the remaining 28 comparisons, no systematic trend emerged. In addition, responses to two abbreviated versions of the New Left scale (Yankelovich-CBS and high school samples) provided further support for the conclusion that there was no relationship between sex and New Left political attitudes.

AGE AND YEAR IN SCHOOL

In the samples of 4-year college students, we found no relationship between age or year in school and scores on the attitude scales. This was true within individual college samples (New York University, Columbia, Oregon State) as well as within the national sample collected by Yankelovich. This finding interested us since it seemed highly plausible that radicalization among students was a result of socializing forces on campuses, a hypothesis that would lead to the expectation that older students would be more radical than younger ones.

Among samples composed of individuals outside the normal college age range, however, a definite pattern emerged: The older respondents were more conservative than the younger ones. At Corning Community College those over 23 years scored significantly lower on the Revolutionary Tactics scale. The over-30 social work students scored significantly higher on Traditional Moralism, and over-30 members of the private school faculty scored significantly lower on Machiavellian Cynicism than their under-30 counterparts. The relationship is most clearly illustrated among a sample of nonstudents gathered by employment counselors in a graduate seminar (Figure 6.2). In fulfilling a course requirement, each class member administered the New Left scale to four acquaintances selected to represent a diversity of age levels and educational backgrounds. Those under 30 scored significantly higher on Machiavellian Cynicism and Revolutionary Tactics and significantly lower on Traditional Moralism. Even when differences in education were controlled, the respondents under 30 were significantly more radical. Recall also that Columbia College panel members were more radical than their parents on four of the five scales (see Chapter 5).

EDUCATIONAL LEVEL ATTAINED

It was possible to examine the relationship between level of education attained and political attitudes in two adult samples—the New York City adults and the parents of the Columbia panel sample. (The other adult sample was composed of school teachers, all with college degrees.) Past research has suggested that formal education is positively correlated with liberal political views; this finding was

[2] Fordham School of Social Work: males higher than females on Traditional Moralism; New York University: females higher than males on New Left Philosophy.

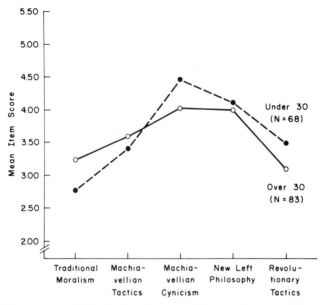

Figure 6.2. Comparison of New Left scale scores of respondents over 30 years old with those under 30 (New York City adult sample).

replicated in the two samples. As shown in Figure 6.3, those respondents with some college education scored significantly lower on the Traditional Moralism scale than those with a high school diploma or less. The trend was highly linear—the greater the amount of education, the less the acceptance of traditional values; and it held when age of respondent was controlled. Significant relationships, all in the same direction, were also found for fathers of the panel sample on the New Left Philosophy scale and for the New York City adults on the Machiavellian Tactics, Machiavellian Cynicism, and Revolutionary Tactics scales.

RELIGION

The relationship between religious preference and New Left attitudes was tested in seven samples (Columbia psychology, Corning, Suffolk, New York University, New York City adults, Fordham Social Work, and private school teachers). Before examining the differences between respondents who professed a religion and those who professed none, we studied differences among respondents who reported they were members of the three major faiths. Typically, Catholics have been found to be the most politically conservative, Protestants to be moderate, and Jews the most politically liberal; but this pattern did not hold

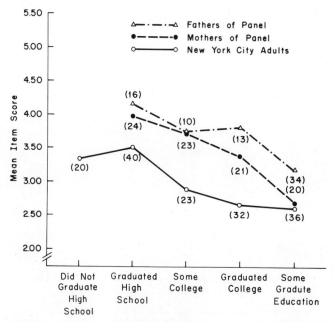

Figure 6.3. Scores on the Traditional Moralism scale by educational level (two adult samples). (For parents of the panel sample, the graduated high school category also includes those who did not graduate high school because there are so few in the latter group.)

for the five student samples from which we collected data; there were no significant differences between any of the faiths.

However, in the Yankelovich college study, Jews were found to be significantly more radical on the abbreviated New Left scale than were Catholics or Protestants, whose scores were almost identical (See Figure 6.4). The difference between the findings of our samples and those of the nationwide survey may be due to the aberrant distribution of religious affiliations present in the seven groups we sampled. An examination of Table 6.2 indicates that the proportion of self-defined Protestants varied from 3% at Columbia to 45% at Corning Community College, that of Catholics from zero among the school faculty to 53% of the social work students from Fordham, and that of Jews from zero at Suffolk Community College to 46% among the New York City adult sample. A comparison of these data with known census figures (and the Yankelovich distribution) indicates that these samples have markedly fewer Protestants than would be found in a national sample. Therefore, the Yankelovich data showing Jewish college students as more radical probably represents a more accurate picture of religious differences than do our data.

Whether the small differences among college students of the three major faiths

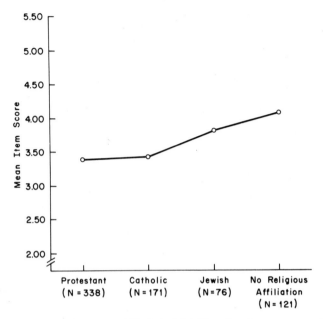

Figure 6.4. New Left scale scores of Yankelovich-CBS national survey respondents, classified by religious affiliation. (Based on a 15-item version of the New Left scale.)

Table 6.2
Religious Affiliation of Respondents in Seven Samples (Expressed as Percentages)[a]

	N	Protestant	Catholic	Jewish	No affiliation
Columbia (psychology class)	110	3	16	24	46
New York University	214	7	22	27	32
Corning Community College	66	49	29	2	17
Suffolk Community College	68	24	47	0	23
Fordham School of Social Work	161	14	49	10	20
New York City adults	151	17	23	44	11
Private school faculty	51	10	8	22	57

[a]Percentage of "no answers" and "other" not included in table.

in our samples (especially between Catholics and Protestants) can be generalized to adults is open to question. An internal analysis of the New York City adult sample revealed a trend relevant to this question. The sample was divided into two age groups, under 30 and over 30, and the differences between each religion were examined separately according to age. Among the younger group no differences were found, but among those over 30 the pattern was as expected: Catholics were generally more conservative than Protestants, who were generally more conservative than Jews. The differences were significant on the Traditional Moralism scale ($F = 3.14$, $df = 2,69$, $p < .05$), and in the predicted direction on the other scales. The data from the Traditional Moralism Scale are shown in Figure 6.5.

When we examined differences between those professing identification with a major faith and those claiming no religious preference, more systematic relationships emerged. The scores of those respondents without a religious affiliation were closer to the protester's profile than were the scores of individuals with a religious affiliation (see Table 6.3). Nonreligious groups tended to score high on Machiavellian Cynicism, New Left Philosophy, and Revolutionary Tactics, and low on Traditional Moralism and Machiavellian Tactics. This pattern was significant in most college samples, but not, interestingly enough, in either of the two adult samples.

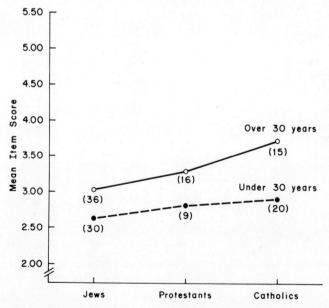

Figure 6.5. Traditional Moralism scores of Catholics, Protestants, and Jews (New York City adult sample).

Table 6.3

Comparison of New Left Scale Scores of Respondents Affiliated with a Major Faith and Respondents Reporting No Religious Affiliation

Sample	N	Traditional Moralism	Machiavellian Tactics	Machiavellian Cynicism	New Left Philosophy	Revolutionary Tactics
			Affiliated with a major faith			
College						
Columbia (psychology class)	47	2.81[a]	3.50[a]	3.86[a]	3.90	3.02[a]
New York University	119	3.25[a]	3.57[a]	4.24	3.87	2.99[a]
Corning Community College	52	3.19[a]	3.34	3.94	3.87[a]	3.07
Suffolk Community College	48	3.52[a]	3.54	3.94[a]	3.74	2.80
Fordham School of Social Work	118	3.22[a]	3.10	3.82[a]	3.71	3.22[a]
Adult						
New York City adults	126	3.06	3.57	4.11	4.11[a]	3.23
Private school faculty	20	2.68	3.13	4.04	3.68	3.37

[a]$p < .05$, t test between respondents who reported affiliation and those within that sample reporting none.

Table 6.3 (continued)

Sample	N	Traditional Moralism	Machiavellian Tactics	Machiavellian Cynicism	New Left Philosophy	Revolutionary Tactics
College		No religious affiliation				
Columbia (psychology class)	50	1.95	3.17	4.43	4.44	4.38
New York University	69	2.31	3.29	4.29	4.23	3.45
Corning Community College	11	2.38	2.96	4.23	4.42	3.27
Suffolk Community College	15	2.86	4.01	4.62	3.95	2.74
Fordham School of Social Work	32	2.43	3.15	4.12	3.88	3.74
Adult						
New York City adults	17	2.90	3.32	4.27	3.54	3.52
Private school faculty	29	2.67	2.97	3.98	3.92	3.37

It has been suggested that the higher degree of radicalism among students with no religious preference can be accounted for primarily by the fact that the majority are from families of Jewish background, who, as discussed earlier, are typically more liberal. Our data do not support such a contention. For example, of the 78 students in the New York University sample who reported no religious affiliation only 19 (24%) had Jewish parents; the rest were fairly evenly distributed among parents of the other major faiths, parents with no church membership, and those with mixed marriages (of which only one-quarter involved Jews).

Discussion

A recurrent theme in the preceding analyses is the difference between older and younger respondents. The attitudinal "drift" from generation to generation, which was seen in the data between parents and their children in the previous chapter, was replicated in several of the noncollege samples, corroborating the significance of the oft-quoted New Left slogan: "Never trust anyone over thirty." But the generational differences appear to run deeper, particularly with respect to religion. Among adults, political attitudes varied according to which of the three major faiths they embraced but not according to whether or not they belonged to one of the major faiths. The opposite pattern was true of college students. Such data suggest that the political meaning of religion differs for the two age groups. The era in which the adult respondents grew up was characterized by relevant distinctions among the faiths, especially as they reflected the ethnic backgrounds of immigrants. Today we are witnessing an ecumenicalism in American religious life, which has perhaps made the crucial question for youth not whether they will choose Catholicism or Protestantism but whether they will choose any religion affiliation at all. Such a decision becomes highly charged with political meaning within the context of the New Left movement, whose main thrust has been a break with the status quo. A youth's rejection of the institution of religion may be symbolic of his rejection of traditional American values in a manner that was not true of his parents' generation.

Summary

In a search for correlates of radicalism, various academic variables (attitudes toward science, scholastic performance, choice of college major, and academic survival) and demographic variables (sex, age, educational level, and religion) were explored. As in the previous chapter, age was found to be negatively related to endorsement of New Left beliefs. Students who reported having a nonpragmatic approach toward college and those who did not identify with an established religion were more likely to exhibit the protester's profile. The stereotypes of radicals as more antiscience, intelligent, and likely to drop out of school were not supported. Relationships between radical attitudes, on the one hand, and educational level and religion, on the other, suggest generational differences analogous to those discussed in the previous chapter.

7

The Social Context

The two preceding chapters have described the lack of relationship of the New Left scales to basic demographic and sociological variables that had previously been found (or been assumed) to be related to political attitudes. The results were preponderantly nonsignificant. Yet we knew from examining the distributions of scores that there was a wide divergence of opinion on the scales, both within samples and between them, and we knew from examining the data on protest activities that the distribution of values was not random but was strongly related to political behavior. Therefore, we decided to look elsewhere for relationships, to analyze the effect of a person's context, or immediate surround, on his/her political attitudes.

Let us recapitulate our findings thus far, so that the development of our interest in contextual variables is clear. The attitudes measured by the New Left scales did not seem to be related to variables that sociologists call "ascribed"— ascribed in the sense that the individual has little or no choice in determining their nature. We found no differences between the sexes on the specifically political scales. Intelligence, as measured by SAT scores, did not seem to discriminate those endorsing New Left beliefs from those who did not, although this relationship was tested only in a relatively homogeneous sample. In addition, and probably most important, none of the variables referring directly to the parents of the respondents—parental socioeconomic status, parental religion, or parental ideological beliefs—were found to be systematically related to the attitudes studied. On the other hand, the significant correlates of radicalism were political activities (whether one had or had not participated in protest demonstrations), choice of religion (whether one did or did not belong to a major faith), educational level attained (whether one had or had not attended college), and educational goals (whether one had a pragmatic or liberal arts philosophy)—all variables that cannot be considered ascribed. Rather, these variables seem to reflect personal involvement, an individual's own method of relating to basic societal institutions, and, as such, they can be construed as representing aspects of the immediate *context* or social environment within which an individual lives. They can be the result of conscious choice or of imposition by others; what is crucial is that they have an import for one's day-to-day life.

Age was the one variable traditionally considered ascribed that was significantly correlated with radicalism. Respondents under 30 were more prone to endorse New Left attitudes than their older counterparts. In an attempt to reconcile this relationship with the interpretation of the data outlined here, we began to rethink the meaning of the age variable. There has recently been a great deal of discussion about a "generation gap" between today's youth and their parents. If we accept that there is a culture and way of thinking characteristic of the under-30 set that is qualitatively different from that of people over 30, then differences in age would be indicative of differences in the "atmosphere" in which one lives. Hence, age could well be considered a contextual variable in the sense we are describing here. Braungart (1974) presents a similar analysis of age differences using Mannheim's concept of generational unit. It was these considerations that led us to analyze the data presented in this chapter.

We perceived two ways of examining the effect of social context. First, we could continue to look at the individual level. What are the variables that differentiate the life style and interpersonal relations of radicals from those of conservatives? For a second approach we could explore the impact of institutions themselves, in this case the most relevant and immediate being the university. This approach focuses on discovering an atmosphere or environmental press that exists above and beyond the distribution of attitudes at the school and affects the beliefs of the people it surrounds.

Before presenting the data, we must emphasize the impossibility of dealing adequately with cause and effect relationships. A person's attitudes undoubtedly influence his life style and the institutions with which he associates. A high school senior who considers himself/herself a radical is more likely to choose a college with a reputation for leftist political activity than is a senior who identifies with the conservative group Young Americans for Freedom. But in either case the institutional environment and personal life style in which the person is embedded or to which he/she is attracted can themselves modify attitudes, and such changes, in turn, may lead the person to seek out new contexts. It is precisely because these forces are interacting that the distinction between what is cause and what is effect is obscured.

Correlates of Radicalism on the Interpersonal Level

One of the first aspects of life style that we examined was students' use of leisure time and the nature of their extracurricular activities. The data were gathered during a friendship study of Columbia College freshmen based on interviews with a 52-member sample, all of whom had taken some form of the New Left scale. The students were questioned about their experiences at Columbia, an average interview lasting about 1 hour. For the analysis, the respondents were divided into three groups—radical, moderate, and conservative—according to their scores on a short version of the scale (see Chapter 3).

There were a number of differences between conservatives and radicals. Predictably, involvement in campus extracurricular activities was along political lines. Radicals belonged to left-wing political organizations, conservatives to right-wing ones. Radicals participated more often in Columbia's "chic" clubs—drama and film; conservatives joined the college band and student government.

Similar differences were found for other leisure time preferences. When radicals attended concerts, which they did as frequently as conservatives, 80% chose to hear rock musicians; the preference of conservatives, however, was for classical music and ballet. Movie interests fell into a similar dichotomy. Political attitudes were not related to number of movies seen but to the nature of the movie. A majority of radical students liked foreign "art" films, yet not one conservative expressed such a preference. We also asked the students about their reading habits. About one-half of the respondents from each of the groups said they had read nothing during the semester other than assigned class readings. Among the other half, 45% of the radicals told us they read spy stories, comic books, and science fiction—the latest youth cult fads. All the conservatives expressed a preference for nonfiction or novels. In addition, although both groups read major newspapers and news magazines (e.g., *New York Times, Newsweek, Time*), only radicals read newspapers and magazines with an anti-Establishment orientation, such as *The Village Voice, Rat,* and *Ramparts.*

In sum, it appears (and not surprisingly so) that radicals and conservatives from the class of 1972 coexisted in two separate social worlds during the spring of their freshman year at Columbia. One world was strongly oriented toward left-wing politics and the "youth cult," the other toward traditional, Establishment pursuits.

In order to check on the validity of the above findings in a more heterogeneous population, we asked high school students to name the radio station to which they preferred listening. The stations were then classified by four judges (our research assistants) into four categories, which varied along a "sophistication," "with-it-ness," or "cosmopolitan" continuum. At the low end of the scale were the AM stations with their popular music and rock-'n'-roll fare; at the other extreme were the FM stations specializing in esoteric black jazz and "acid rock." A comparison of the New Left scale scores of the students listening to stations in each of the categories is shown in Figure 7.1. As expected, individuals who listened to the most sophisticated stations endorsed more radical beliefs than those who preferred less sophisticated stations ($F = 7.8, df = 3,191, p < .01$).

Friendships and peer groups are another important contextual consideration. While friends are often chosen on the basis of compatibility of value systems (Lazarsfeld & Merton, 1954; Newcomb, 1961), they often influence one another's values. In studies of voting behavior, changes in choice of candidates appeared most often to be due to pressure from family and friends (Lazarsfeld, Berelson, & Gaudet, 1968). Such influence is not limited to elections. Barton (1972) reports that the attitudes of friends played a central role in determining reactions to the demonstrations on the Columbia campus in 1968. For example, he found that 60% of self-proclaimed left-wing Columbia students whose friends supported the sit-ins also supported the sit-ins, but only 12% of the self-pro-claimed left-wing students whose friends were opposed to the sit-ins supported them. Two years later, about one-half of our sample of Columbia College sophomores cited friends as the most important influence on their political attitudes since beginning college. None of the other alternatives—parents, politi-

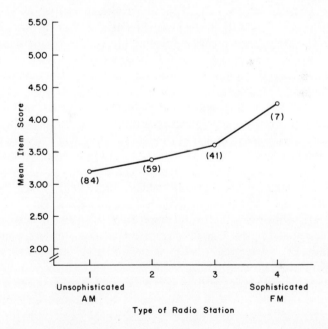

Figure 7.1. Abbreviated New Left scale scores of high school students, by sophistication of radio station preferred. (Based on a 30-item version of the revised New Left scale.)

cal participation, communications media, books, or teachers—was cited as often as friends.

Because of the apparent importance of interpersonal influence at Columbia and elsewhere, we decided to examine the friendship patterns among students of varying political beliefs. We hoped such an analysis would help delineate further the differences in the social contexts of conservative and radical students.

The relevant data again come from the friendship study of 52 Columbia freshmen. Each of the interviewees was asked to name all the people he considered "close friends" while at college. Of the 234 friends named, 121 had taken a version of the New Left scale. In Table 7.1 the political classification of interviewees is tallied against the political classification of their friends, using the same tripartite division of attitudes as we did with life styles.

The tendency for persons to choose friends with attitudes similar to their own is highly significant. While this is not surprising, two points should be emphasized—the near perfect symmetry of the frequencies and the fact that two of the three cases that spanned the radical-conservative continuum were high school friendships. In other words, in only *one* instance out of 121 did two people of opposing political beliefs become friends while at Columbia.

Since the relationships among close friends proved to be highly contingent upon political attitudes, we looked further into the patterning of acquaintance networks. Did the extreme radicals and the extreme conservatives at Columbia *know* each other? And if so how would one describe the matrix of such linkages? The analysis was guided by Kadushin's research on the social circle, a concept originally proposed by Simmel. A social circle refers to a loose urban social unit having the following three characteristics: (1) common interests, rather than propinquity, as the basis of interaction, (2) a lack of formal organization and leadership, and (3) an indirect chain of interaction (i.e., not everyone knows everyone else, but all are linked through some third party in the circle) (Kadushin, 1966). We expected that students with extreme but similar political values would know each other and would be organized in two social circles—one being comprised of the radicals and the other of the conservatives.

In the first stage of the friendship study, 19 freshmen from the original 153-member panel sample were approached for interviews. They were selected on the basis of their New Left scale scores from the previous fall—7 of the 10 most radical students, the 7 most conservative, and 5 scoring at the mean of the distribution. Each was given a list of names of the 19 students (including the respondent's own name) and asked to indicate whom he knew and the degree of friendship.[1] A sociometric matrix was created from these data, linking any two

---

[1] The interviewer was unable to contact two of the seven radicals, and hence they were never interviewed. Their names, however, appeared on the list.

Table 7.1
Political Attitudes of Respondents in Columbia Friendship
Study, by Political Attitudes of Close Friends

	Friends			
Respondent	Conservative	Moderate	Radical	Total
Conservative	15	12	1	28[a]
Moderate	12	25	10	47
Radical	2	19	25	46
Totals	29	56	36	121

[a]This total is low because conservatives in the sample had
more upperclassmen as friends than did the other two groups.
No upperclassmen took the scale.

students between whom there existed at least a talking relationship (i.e., more than nodding acquaintanceship).

The pattern that emerged supported the prediction that individuals with extreme political views would tend to be acquainted with others with similar views. In addition, the pattern of the networks resembled that of the social circle, being characterized by indirect, rather than direct, interaction. Among the radicals while only two of the seven were good friends, five were linked in a chainlike fashion; the other two were isolates (i.e., knew no one on the list). Of the seven conservatives, six were similarly linked, the remaining student being connected to the other conservatives through an acquaintanceship with one of the moderates. However, not one of the five moderates knew another moderate, although they did know many of the radicals and conservatives. The data are perhaps best conceptualized as reflecting grapevines or rumor transmission mechanisms. Imagine that some piece of information is given to one member of each of the three groups (radicals, moderates, and conservatives); that member is then told to convey the information to another person in his group whom he knows, who in turn must convey it to one of his friends in the group, and so on. Given the networks we found, it would be possible for five of the seven radicals and six of the seven conservatives to receive the information eventually; but the information could never get past the initial moderate transmitter—he knows no other moderate to whom he can transmit it.

What seemed to us most compelling about the findings presented thus far was the strength of the relationships uncovered. In contrast to the few significant but weak tendencies found in connection with parental, background, and academic variables, the differences in life style and interpersonal relations between radicals and conservatives were sharp and highly significant.

Correlates of Radicalism at the Institutional Level

FORMAL CHARACTERISTICS OF INSTITUTIONS:
ELITENESS AND THE POLITICAL ATTITUDES OF STUDENTS

Our initial assumption was that there would be a positive relationship between the eliteness of a college or university and the extent to which its students were in dissent. There were a number of reasons for making such an assumption, aside from the fact that most of the highly publicized early incidents occurred at such high-status schools as Berkeley, Chicago, Wisconsin, and Columbia. First, the pre-1968 findings about the relationship between parental status and student dissent meant that those who could pay the high fees required by private colleges came largely from such families. The more prestigious state universities also tended to screen students on such criteria as aptitude test scores and high school grades, both of which have been found to be empirically correlated with family status. Other reasons were based on more contextual variables. We suspected there might be a different emphasis in the course work at a prestigious liberal arts school compared with a school concerned primarily with mastering technical and vocational skills. One of the supposed functions of a liberal education is an informed critical orientation toward life and society; that of a more vocationally oriented education is preparation for a place within the established order. We also assumed that faculties at more affluent schools would be more likely to be liberal, and in some cases dissenting, than those at less distinguished schools. While it is, of course, a moot point how much direct influence professors have on students, they do form a significant part of any collegiate environment. The fact that more prestigious schools are more tolerant of professors' dissent than less prestigious ones is an indication of a less restrictive atmosphere.

The availability of the Yankelovich-CBS data afforded us an opportunity to check this relationship. The samples had been selected to represent the spectrum of American colleges. Although the number of schools was small (we used 29 of the 30), it covered a wide range of institutions. Harvard, for example, listed 1 faculty member for every 2 students, whereas Nassau Community College had 1 faculty member per 450 students.

We used a composite of five characteristics to determine eliteness of school, because no single indicator was adequate. For example, some of the persons listed as faculty by Harvard probably had no personal contact with students, whereas it is difficult to see how any professor at Nassau could avoid it. The five classificatory indices were based on the following ratios:

Number of faculty/Number of students
Number of books in library/Number of students
Annual operating budget/Number of students

Number of scholarship students/Number of students
Number of faculty with Ph.D.s/Number of faculty

These five indicators were found by Astin (1962) to load highest on the first factor analysis of all available data on 315 colleges. He dubbed the factor "affluence."

The 29 schools were ranked on each characteristic, and the rank scores on each of the five indicators were then summed and the sums ranked. A rank-order correlation was then computed between the composite rank of the school by the ranked index of its students' radical attitudes (described in Appendix B-3). Contrary to our expectations, the rank-order correlation was a nonsignificant +.03.

One possible reason for the lack of a relationship is that the sample of respondents within individual schools was nonrepresentative of the student body. As a check, the respondents in various schools were examined to determine their composition in terms of background variables. The samples from most schools seemed reasonably representative, from what could be inferred from available data on student and institutional characteristics. For only two schools did there appear to be a nonrepresentative distribution of students; certainly these discrepancies were not sufficient to account for the lack of correlation.

A second step was to examine the correlation plot and to check on individual schools to see if there were any other factors that might account for the failure to find the predicted result. This plot is reproduced in Figure 7.2. Certain schools fall very close to the predicted diagonal line, such as Harvard (5) and Berkeley (4), which were high in both affluence and radicalism, and Elmira (20) (a private school in upstate New York), Del Mar (26) (a junior college in Corpus Christi, Texas), and McNeese (29) (a state college in Louisiana), which had low ranks on both indicators.

Five schools had high positive discrepancy scores between eliteness and radicalism (upper left quadrant). Furman (28) and Hanover (24) are both small Protestant-affiliated colleges located in geographically remote areas of western North Carolina and southeastern Indiana, respectively. Arkansas (27) and Nebraska (22) are both middle-sized state universities and again somewhat isolated from major metropolitan areas. Minnesota (23), is one of the two schools noted earlier where sampling appeared nonrepresentative.

The cluster of six schools in the lower right quadrant, which were low on affluence and high on radicalism, also violated expectations based on an eliteness hypothesis. Four of the six are junior colleges located in large metropolitan areas: Los Angeles City (6) and Rio Hondo (10) in Whittier are both in the Los Angeles metropolitan area, Delta (9) is in the Detroit metropolitan area, and Nassau (12) is in Garden City just across the New York City line. Central State (1) differs from the other colleges in the sample in being predominantly black and also the first college (in this sample) to have an active SDS chapter (Sale, 1973). Also of

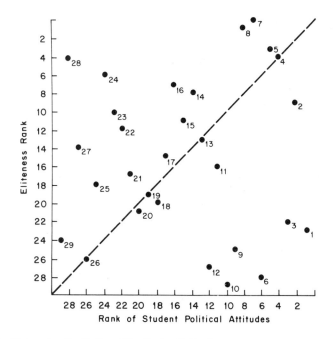

Figure 7.2. Scatter plot of 29 schools, comparing eliteness index with political attitudes index.

KEY: (U = University; C = College; JC = Junior College)

1. (C) Central State (Ohio)
2. (U) Wisconsin (Madison)
3. (C) Western Washington State
4. (U) California (Berkeley)
5. (U) Harvard (Massachusetts)
6. (JC) Los Angeles City
7. (C) Amherst (Massachusetts)
8. (U) Rochester (New York)
9. (JC) Delta (Michigan)
10. (JC) Rio Hondo (California)
11. (U) George Washington (D.C.)
12. (JC) Nassau Community (New York)
13. (U) Pittsburgh (Pennsylvania)
14. (U) Rhode Island
15. (U) Kansas State

16. (C) Asheville-Biltmore (North Carolina)
17. (JC) St. Gregory (Oklahoma)
18. (U) Arizona State
19. (U) Missouri (Kansas City)
20. (C) Elmira (New York)
21. (C) Portland State (Oregon)
22. (U) Nebraska (Lincoln)
23. (U) Minnesota (Minneapolis)
24. (C) Hanover (Indiana)
25. (C) Walla Walla (Washington)
26. (JC) Del Mar (Texas)
27. (U) Arkansas (Fayetteville)
28. (U) Furman (South Carolina)
29. (C) McNeese State (Louisiana)

importance is the fact that there had been a number of overt clashes between students and administration. Although Central State is not located in a cosmopolitan area (Wilberforce, Ohio), many of its students came from urban backgrounds. The remaining college in this group, Western Washington State (3) in Bellingham had an active SDS chapter in 1965, and had had a major confrontation over the Reserve Officers' Training Corps (ROTC) building.

This analysis suggests that, although the eliteness of the college may have influenced students' attitudes, its role was not that important in the spring of 1969. Neither did the size of the institution have an observable effect according to the data. The only conclusion we could draw was that schools geographically isolated and at which there had been no known major confrontations were most likely to have a low radicalism index score, regardless of their elite qualities. In a general sense it would seem that the level of radical attitudes at a particular school was positively related to the exposure of students to the broader youth counterculture of the 1960s. Data on informal characteristics of institutions to be presented later in the chapter support such an explanation.

SOCIOECONOMIC STATUS AND THE ACTIVISM OF STUDENTS

The ranked index of institutional eliteness was run against the ranked index of the mean of self-reported activism on the part of the students at each school (see Appendix D). The correlation was low. +.15, but was a bit higher than the +.03 we had found with radical attitudes. The activism index also correlated with parental income to the same degree. Parental income correlated with eliteness of the schools, +.48, although there was some evidence of a curvilinear relationship.

This set of relationships was interesting enough to examine further. We therefore divided the schools into three groups—high, medium, and low activist according to the mean reported activities of students—and examined the relationship between parental income and student activism within each group. The data are plotted in Figure 7.3. In both high and low activism schools the relationship is a curvilinear one. Those reporting parental income within the $10,000 to $15,000 range were less likely to engage in protest activities than those from families with a lower or higher income. This suggests—but only suggests—that students from poor families as well as those from affluent families feel less constrained from engaging in protest activities than do those from middle-income families.

There are two reasons for reporting these data, flawed as they are by basing both the school's radicalism and individual activism on the same set of data. One is that the curvilinear relationship between family income and student activism parallels a similar finding by Somers (1965) in a study at Berkeley. The second is the paucity of positive findings in our data relating either institutional or familial variables to student protest, which makes even a suggestive finding seem worthy of some consideration.

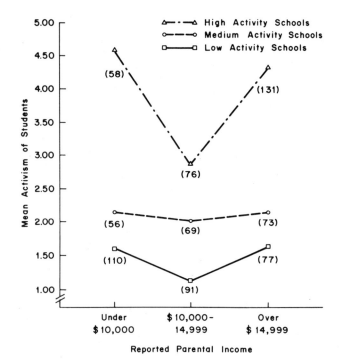

Figure 7.3. Relationship between student activism and parental income in high, medium, and low activist schools.

INFORMAL CHARACTERISTICS OF INSTITUTIONS:
INSTITUTIONAL ENVIRONMENT AND
POLITICAL ATTITUDES OF STUDENTS

So far in this analysis of the correlates of radicalism at the institutional level, we have dealt with the formal characteristics of relative eliteness of the institution. We now turn to those institutional characteristics that more immediately shape the social environment or social context of those who are associated with it.

In our earlier analysis of the correlation between a school's eliteness rank and its rank on our measure of New Left ideology from the Yankelovich research, we noted important informal characteristics of institutions that appeared to affect attitudes—the school's location (urban versus nonurban) and its history of campus dissent. When we examined differences in New Left scale scores among our own group of samples we were struck by the similarity of findings. Figure 7.4 presents the means on the 30-item abbreviated version of the New Left scale for

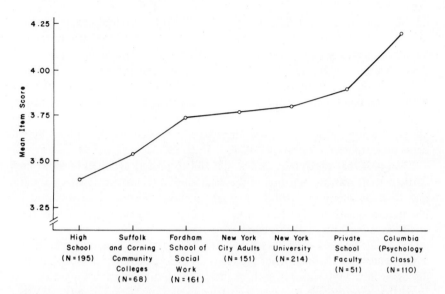

Figure 7.4. Abbreviated New Left scale scores for all samples administered the revised scale.

samples administered the revised form.[2] The scores range from 3.4 at the high school to 4.2 at Columbia College, a highly significant difference. But the means also tend to fall into three distinct "environmental" clusters. The first, the least radical, includes the high school students and students at the two community colleges. The second encompasses members of most of the other samples—Fordham School of Social Work students, those interviewed by the New York State Employment counselors, New York University undergraduates, and members of the faculty at a New York City private school. The third consists only of the Columbia College psychology class. These three clusters—like the clustering of institutional eliteness-political attitude scores among various colleges in the national sample—seem to reflect a continuum of such factors as exposure to the forces of urban living, encounters with dissatisfied members of society, and confrontation experience with police. For example, the high school and community college samples were located in nonurban settings and had little contact, except through the media, with potentially politicizing influences. No major confrontation of students with administration or with police had occurred either at these institutions or in neighboring towns. This lack of face-to-face exposure seems a probable reason for the relatively conservative attitude of their students. The

---

[2] Use of the 30-item version of the revised New Left scale permits the largest number of comparisons of scores.

opposite conditions held for members of the Columbia College sample, the most radical. Not only did they live in New York City in close proximity to the Harlem community, but the majority were freshmen at Columbia during the major demonstrations in the spring of 1968. All the samples from the middle cluster were from the New York City area. The work of the Fordham students, the New York State Employment counselors, and the progressive private school faculty revolved around social services that brought them into daily contact with urban minority groups. New York University had experienced demonstrations by students protesting administration policy.

We suggest that exposure to urban life and to protest activities (even without participation) was instrumental in the creation of a radical atmosphere (or informal context) within an institution which, in turn, affected the attitudes of the institution's members. Let us turn to an analysis of the data from some of those institutions for support of this hypothesis.

One of the primary concerns of the interview study of Columbia freshmen was with friendship networks. After interviewees had named their close friends they discussed how they had met each of them. The results from this question indicated that most people had met their friends because of propinquity, i.e., they lived on the same dormitory floor (see Table 7.2). But this pattern of friendship formation was not politically random. Of the 14 conservatives in the sample who lived in the dorms, only 7 had made a close friend living on the same floor, as contrasted with all of the moderates and 13 of the 16 radicals. Only 4 of the 12 conservatives living in double rooms or suites considered their roommates as friends, while 10 of 16 moderates and 11 of 16 radicals did so. These differences cannot be accounted for by differences in absolute numbers of friends. Members of all three political groups reported the same mean number of friends. Conservatives tended to meet their friends through channels other than propinquity—particularly through extracurricular activities.

Table 7.2
How Columbia Freshmen Met Their Close Friends

Method	Percentage of sample having met at least one friend in category	Total number of friends in category	Percentage of total friends
Floor of dormitory	79[a]	100[a]	43[a]
Hometown	46	38	16
College classes	46	33	14
Through other friends	38	27	12
Extracurricular interest groups	29	36	15

[a]Does not include the four sample members living off campus.

The data just presented are intriguing because the pattern of results for radicals and moderates was very similar; both differed from that of the conservatives. Such a pattern may be explained by examining the relationship of the conservative Columbia freshman to the rest of the Columbia student body. At the time of the study the campus was politically polarized. The dominant culture was radical. In fact, most sophomores in the class of 1972 sample rated themselves as more radical than their friends. Conservatives were conspicuously deviant. This point is nicely illustrated by an advertisement that appeared in the Columbia *Spectator,* the student newspaper: "Do you feel like a member of a minority group? Come to the meeting of the Young Republicans tonight." Because of such an environment, conservatives probably found it more difficult to make friends. They were less likely to find their roommates and other students living on the floor politically compatible. Therefore they had to go outside, to extracurricular activities, to find people with attitudes and interests similar to their own.

This suggests how the atmosphere on a college campus can influence the behavior of its students. So far, however, we have discussed data that are only indirectly political and do not strictly speak to the proposed impact of context on political *attitudes.* For more direct evidence, we turn to a study done by Zweigenhaft comparing responses from Columbia and Corning Community College (see Appendix A). He asked respondents to indicate how much they liked a fictitious college senior who was presented to them either as a draft resister or as an army enlistee. In addition, each respondent rated himself on a 7-point bipolar adjective scale, the end points of which were dove (1) and hawk (7). Corning and Columbia students were then matched for their self-rating on this scale, and the degree of liking of the fictitious senior by those calling themselves doves (scale points 2 and 3) and by those calling themselves hawks (scale points 5 and 6) was compared. The data indicated that a person's own attitude (dove versus hawk) was *not* related to a preference for the resister or for the enlistee. However, the college that a person attended was so related. Columbia students, regardless of their self-rating, preferred the resister to the enlistee; Corning students, on the other hand, preferred the enlistee. Being enrolled at these different institutions (Columbia versus Corning) had a greater impact on their attitudes toward a draft resister than did personal political beliefs.

Discussion

It seems to us that during the spring of 1969 the relevant social environment for most college students was largely one composed of an informal network of friends with similar values. A primary basis for attraction to or rejection of peers, we would further argue, was the extent to which fellow students were involved in the pattern of life style variables associated with the New Left. The particular educational institution in which students were enrolled, served as the nexus for the patterns of interpersonal connections, but formal institutional characteristics were less important than the environment of the institution and the extent to which members of the student body were plugged into the youth counterculture.

How students became plugged into the youth counterculture is difficult to pinpoint, but the process clearly cut across the formal demographic categories frequently used in analyses of social movements. There are several reasons why such categories were not relevant. The student generation of the late 1960s was the first to be weaned on television, a medium that transcends geographic and social class boundaries within the United States. A mass youth market developed, so that young people in widely varying social environments shared a common exposure to attitudes and values. To an unprecedented extent, there was rapid diffusion of a new life style. Aside from the common elements spread by the mass media, there was also geographic mobility, spawned partly by special youth fares and less restrictive parents, and made possible by greater affluence.

During the 1960s, the increasing politicization of the young generation was one of these new elements that spread rapidly across the nation. Protests by students in such places as the Bay Area (particularly at Berkeley), at the universities of Wisconsin, Chicago, and Michigan, and at universities in New York and Cambridge, Massachusetts, spread quickly to schools in more remote areas. The electronic media carried the message, and the participants in those events traveled from one campus to another, sharing their experiences.

This diffusion of protest can be illustrated by two examples. Sale (1973) has pointed out that most of the founders and early members of SDS up to 1965 closely fit the description of the pre-1968 college radical—from relatively well-to-do urban families with a history of liberal or radical political involvement, and intellectually as well as idealistically motivated. However, from 1965 on, the leadership became dominated by exemplars of "prairie power," and the largely northeastern-based early leaders were superseded by mid-western populists with an emphasis on radical action rather than radical theorizing.

Similarly, the broadening base of protest was graphically portrayed in the shifting constituencies of the antiwar demonstrations in Washington, D.C. The Pentagon march of 1967 was composed predominantly of radicals from New York labor unions and the vanguard of the New Left members from such schools as Columbia. Two years later, in the November 1969 moratorium, banners bore the names of Ivy League schools, prestigious small liberal arts colleges such as Swarthmore, and midwestern bastions of protest such as Chicago, Michigan, and Wisconsin. About 6 months later, at the time of the protest over the Cambodian incursion and Kent State, there were fewer marchers behind the banners of the elite schools, and more marchers from the smaller schools as well as from such disparate groups of the young as Chattanooga against the War and Young Socialists of Norman (Oklahoma).

But *why* the diffusion of dissent? Again, the argument is speculative. Most white college students had grown up in protected enclaves in the suburbs, where they were not exposed to the repressive measures sometimes used in ghetto areas or in the South against blacks. A policeman was extolled in children's books as one who helped people across the street rather than as one who helped maintain a segregationist status quo. Similarly, most were brought up on the notion that the conduct of the United States in international matters was benign and idealistic. Growing exposure on television to the harsher aspects of our involvement in Vietnam and the increasing flow of revelations and confirmations of governmental deception simply did not match the image of America they had imbibed at home and in school. Although it was the more idealistic and intelligent of the younger generation who first perceived a discrepancy between professed American ideals and reality, the events of the 1960s increasingly confirmed such misgivings. Although the spread of protest techniques was in many ways like a fad, we suggest that there would not have been as great or as rapid a diffusion if the reasons for disillusionment had not been based in reality.

Summary

The failure to find meaningful relationships between New Left ideology and such ascribed characteristics as social class, sex, family religion, parental values, and a host of other variables, with the important exception of age, initially puzzled us. When we turned to the context of the youth culture, however, we found a marked contrast; a complex of variables differentiated the life styles of radical and conservative students. The students coexisted in two separate subcultures, and their tastes in reading, music, and other forms of cultural expression reflected that dichotomy. Patterns of friendship and even of acquaintanceship were overwhelmingly within the bounds of the separate life styles preferred by conservatives on the one hand and radicals on the other.

An examination of questionnaire replies by students at a heterogeneous sample of colleges indicated no major relationship between formal institutional characteristics measuring the eliteness of the school and radical ideology. There was, however, evidence of a relationship between more informal characteristics of the institution and ideology. This we attribute to the importance of the peer counterculture, which was fostered and spread by the mass media and by informal friendship and communication networks that transcended individual institutions.

8
The
Radicalization Process

A primary purpose of the research program was to explore the radicalization process. In the past there have been only a few attempts by social scientists to investigate this phenomenon empirically. Keniston (1968) gained insight into the process during intensive interviews with 14 New Left political activists. Barton (1968) tried to assess radicalization during the 1968 Columbia crisis using large-scale survey techniques. Both of these investigators relied on retrospective data; respondents were asked to think back to their earlier experiences and recall their feelings and activities at that time. Such data are frequently imprecise and are often subject to biases. A more appropriate approach may be longitudinal research. In this chapter and the next one we present data on the radicalization process based on a 1-year panel investigation of attitude and behavior change among Columbia College freshmen.

There is a remarkable paucity of longitudinal designs in social psychological literature. Psychologists are often reluctant to use such designs because of the unpredictability of events, which can distort and disrupt data collecting. Our situation, we thought, was different. We believed that external events, even though they could only be documented and not controlled, would benefit the research by their potentially radicalizing effect on students. During the spring of 1968 the Columbia campus had witnessed massive demonstrations against the administration and policies of the university. The changes that the crisis seemed to engender in participants intrigued us. Students who, until then, had rarely been seen attending any of the numerous political rallies held weekly on the Columbia campus suddenly became adamant protesters occupying buildings. We also noted changes in our own political outlook as a result of the protests. These experiences were apparently not idiosyncratic. Retrospective data from an unpublished study of students involved in the demonstrations and counterdemonstrations suggest that the crisis had indeed polarized political attitudes.

The political ambience of the campus pointed to the likelihood of another such crisis or series of crises during the next academic year. It was in anticipation of these protests that the decision to undertake the panel study was made. Unfortunately (for hypothesis testing) no major disruptions occurred. The resignation of Columbia's president, Grayson Kirk, shortly before classes started the following autumn and the efforts of the new administration to calm the campus helped prevent further confrontations. There were, to be sure, attempts by radical students to engage the mass of students, but these were not very successful. We therefore had to content ourselves with studying changes in political attitudes and behavior without the aid of a catalytic upheaval on campus. Our intuition had failed; we fell victims to the risks of longitudinal research from which we had believed ourselves protected.

Although we could not pinpoint specific causes of the radicalization observed, the panel design proved invaluable for exploring other questions. In this chapter we deal with one of them, the stages of the radicalization process itself—what happens during such a process, what attitudes change and what behaviors change. Our focus is not on the process of becoming a radical but on the process of becoming more radical, that is, *radicalized.*

Radicalization 1968-1969

All the data pertaining to radicalization were collected from a panel of 122 Columbia College students of the class of 1972 who completed the New Left scale as well as additional background questionnaires during the fall of their freshman and sophomore years (see Chapter 3 for sampling details). We first examined the overall changes in political attitudes and activities from freshman to sophomore year. Table 8.1 presents the mean change scores of the sample members for the five scales of the New Left scale. On all scales a shift in attitudes in the radical direction was observed. However, this shift was significant only for Revolutionary Tactics ($t=5.30$, $df=120$, $p<.001$). The absolute number of students who became more favorable toward the use of revolutionary tactics was also significantly greater than the number becoming less favorable; 62% shifted in the radical direction, only 13% in the conservative direction ($z=2.45$, $p<.02$).

During a comparable period—from before college to the beginning of sophomore year—participation in political protest activity by panel members increased sharply. When the students first arrived at Columbia, only 34% had been in demonstrations or political confrontations with police; by the fall of their sophomore year 81% reported such involvement. Presumably much of this in-

Table 8.1

Test-Retest Correlations and Change Scores on the New Left Scales for Panel Sample, from Freshman to Sophomore Year (*N*=122)

	Traditional Moralism	Machiavellian Tactics	Machiavellian Cynicism	New Left Philosophy	Revolutionary Tactics
Correlation be-tween freshman and sophomore scores	.71	.54	.57	.64	.66
Attitude change scores (sophomore score minus freshman score)					
X	−.03	−.11	.13	.14	.43
SD	.77	.77	.84	.92	.87

creased involvement can be attributed to the increase in opportunities for such behavior. Antiwar protests were prevalent both in New York City and on the Columbia campus. Several rallies were held in the city for the nationwide Vietnam Moratorium Day on October 15, 1969; 75% of the sample reported attending at least one of the rallies. Almost one-half of the sample went to Washington, D.C., for the anti-Vietnam march a month later. While getting to Washington required effort and commitment, the number of buses chartered by college and community groups (approximately 50) made the event readily accessible for the Columbia student.

In sum, by their second year at Columbia, many of the students in the panel sample had been radicalized. They were more likely to endorse the use of violent means for achieving political change and more likely to have participated in potentially violent types of political activity than they had been upon entering college.

Studying the Change

The large degree of change, both in belief and in behavior, convinced us of the value of using this sample to study the radicalization process. In keeping with an initial theoretical focus and previous research interests, we began the analysis by defining radicalization in terms of change in attitudes rather than change in behavior. Of the possible approaches to the data, we chose proportionate change on the Revolutionary Tactics scale as the dependent variable to indicate radicalization. Several considerations entered into these decisions.

1. Change on one of the attitude scales could be more finely quantified than change on the behavioral scale and hence subjected to more sensitive statistical tests. The wide range of possible attitudinal responses allowed for a greater variability of movement in both the radical and conservative direction than did the limited categories of the activity scale. In addition, the attitude scales had proved to be reliable using both split-half and test-retest methods.

2. The Revolutionary Tactics scale was selected to measure radicalization because it was the scale on which panel members' scores most clearly paralleled their behavior. It best differentiated freshman dissident activists from nonactivists and was the only attitude scale on which scores shifted significantly to the left simultaneously with the significant increase observed in protest activity from freshman to sophomore year. Previous analyses also indicated that Revolutionary Tactics represented the more "radical" attitudes of all the five scales, and it was more likely than any of the other scales to differentiate known conservative groups (e.g., policemen) and radical groups (e.g., members of the Berkeley counterculture) from each other (see Chapter 2).

3. Proportionate shift scores were used instead of absolute change scores to control for ceiling effects due to the finite scale of measurement. They were calculated by determining the amount an individual changed his endorsement of Revolutionary Tactics between freshman and sophomore years as a percentage of possible change on the scale in that direction.

In order to facilitate an understanding of the radicalization process and to satisfy our idiosyncratic preference for visual rather than numerical representation of data, we decided to group the sample members for the statistical analyses. After much debate we settled on six initial groups based on differences in political attitude and level of political activity with which the students had entered college. The panel was therefore first divided according to the standard activity classification—dissident activist, sympathizer, nonactivist. The use of these activity groups allowed comparisons within the framework of the profiles drawn from other samples (cf. Chapter 4). We next divided each of the three activity groups according to initial freshman scores on the Revolutionary Tactics scale. The high groups included those respondents who scored above the median, the low groups included those scoring below the median. The resulting six groups were titled: nonactivist lows, sympathizer lows, dissident activist lows, nonactivist highs, sympathizer highs, and dissident activist highs.

There were two major reasons for classifying the panel members in this way:

1. Since the six groups controlled for freshman levels of political beliefs and activities, we could look at variables associated with radicalization independent of students' initial positions. Our interest was in the phenomenon of increasing belief in radical ideas; we were concerned both with the students who moved

from a relatively conservative to a moderate position as well as with those who moved from moderate or radical to a more radical position.

2. Stratifying the six groups according to attitude and activity levels allowed us to conceptualize the groups as representing different stages in the radicalization process. We could then analyze particular characteristics associated with each step of the process.

In Table 8.2 the mean proportionate change scores for the six groups are presented.[1] The students who scored below the median on the Revolutionary Tactics scale in the fall of their freshman year were more radicalized than those who scored above the median. There were, however, no differences in change scores as a function of precollege activity levels. The mean proportionate change on Revolutionary Tactics of the nonactivists was not greater than that of the sympathizers or dissident activists.

Taking another perspective and examining the percentage of students in each group who increased their endorsement of Revolutionary Tactics yielded results similar to the mean proportionate change data. As can be seen in Table 8.3, 85% of the students who initially scored low on Revolutionary Tactics were radicalized during their freshman year compared to 39% who scored high. The precollege activity level of students was again not a good predictor of whether or not they would be radicalized.

A Description of the Radicalization Process

Before we can understand any change phenomenon, a description of the change process itself is needed. For example, a thorough study of concept learning in children would involve not only an analysis of the factors that facilitate or inhibit such learning but also an analysis of the steps or changes (physiological-cognitive) that occur while the child learns. Studying radicalization is no exception. It requires a knowledge of what it means to the individual to be radicalized. The following discussion is an attempt in this direction.

Let us represent radicalization as a horizontal continuum measuring degree of radicalism, the low end at the left, the high end at the right. (Unfortunately, visual conventions do not match the political ones.) At a particular time an individual can be located at any point on the continuum, that point being more or less defined as his score on the Revolutionary Tactics scale, our best indicator of radicalism. Movement from low to high is indicative of radicalization and, by definition, of increasing endorsement of the use of revolutionary tactics for politi-

---

[1] One student did not answer the activity question and had to be eliminated from all subsequent analyses. Radicalization data are therefore based on a 121-member sample.

Table 8.2
Mean Proportionate Change Scores of Panel Sample on the Revolutionary Tactics Scale for the Six Attitude-Activity Groups

Freshman score on Revolutionary Tactics scale	Prefreshman activity level							
	Nonactivists		Sympathizer		Dissident activists		Total	
	$\bar{X}$	SD	$\bar{X}$	SD	$\bar{X}$	SD	$\bar{X}$	SD
High	−.03	.27	.00	.32	+.02	.29	.00	.29
	(N=21)		(N=13)		(N=28)			
Low	+.13	.15	+.10	.19	+.22	.20	+.14	.18
	(N=26)		(N=20)		(N=13)			
Totals	.02	.22	.06	.25	.08	.28		

cal action. Such movement is also accompanied by other changes on the part of the individual, both attitudinal and behavioral. These changes constitute what we have called the radicalization process. As discussed in the introduction to this chapter, we cannot point to any single event that radicalized the students. Thus, we must content ourselves with being cartographers and merely chart what we see.

We have divided the process into three stages—initial, middle, and final. It should be emphasized that these stages are not meant to represent equal intervals. Also, they correspond only to the radicalization continuum as we were able to observe it. Our sample of Columbia College freshmen did not contain many representatives of the extremes of the political spectrum, such as the conservative John Birch Society members (who would not choose to attend a "radical" school such as Columbia) or the radical Weathermen (who, for the most part, had gone underground). This means that our stages do not reflect true endpoints

Table 8.3
Percentage of Respondents in the Six Attitude-Activity Groups Who Increased Their Endorsement of Revolutionary Tactics

Freshman score on Revolutionary Tactics scale	Prefreshman activity level			
	Nonactivist	Sympathizer	Dissident activist	Total
High	48	15	43	39
Low	85	80	92	85
Totals	67	55	60	62

of the continuum. We begin with a brief presentation of our model of the radicalization process. This is followed by a detailed discussion of the data that led us to postulate such a model.

THE MODEL

The model is an attempt to trace the history of a hypothetical individual as he moves from one end of the continuum to the other, passing through each of the three stages. It is diagrammed in Figure 8.1.

Stage I.   The first step appears to be a change in beliefs about traditional values (the Traditional Moralism scale). An individual becomes less accepting of the status quo and more willing to accept changes that may contradict conventional wisdom. This shift away from traditional values seems necessary for further movement along the continuum.

Stage II.   This stage includes changes in both attitudes and behavior. An individual becomes more likely to believe in the goals of the New Left (New Left Philosophy scale) and more likely to be cynical about either the desire or the ability of people and the government to rectify injustices (Machiavellian Cynicism scale). Simultaneously, the relationship between his/her political attitudes and his/her political behavior becomes more consistent. The farther he/she moves along the continuum (i.e., the more he/she endorses Revolutionary Tactics), the more likely he/she is to increase his/her involvement in confrontation activities.

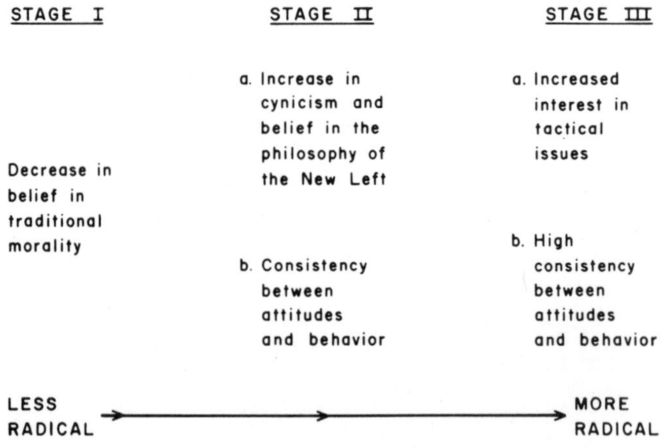

STAGE I	STAGE II	STAGE III
	a. Increase in cynicism and belief in the philosophy of the New Left	a. Increased interest in tactical issues
Decrease in belief in traditional morality		
	b. Consistency between attitudes and behavior	b. High consistency between attitudes and behavior
LESS RADICAL ⟶	⟶	MORE RADICAL

Figure 8.1. Diagram of hypothesized radicalization process.

Stage III. At this stage, political interests change from a primary concern with particular issues to a concern with tactics. Narrow issues, such as the Vietnam War and pollution, no longer dominate. Involvement is in devising tactics to fight the problems of "structural oppression." There also appears to be an increasing need for consistency between beliefs and behavior.

THE DATA

Although the model has been presented from the point of view of a single individual, it was not derived this way. Such a task would have been impossible because we measured a student's attitudes and activities at only two points in time, not the three the creation of such a model would require. The model was actually developed from a comparison of the six groups. On the basis of the levels of political activity and attitudes, each group was placed at one of the three stages on the radicalization continuum, and the differences between groups at the three stages were examined in two ways. First, we compared means across the groups; second, we looked within each group for differences between individuals who became radicalized and individuals who did not.[2]

Based on an inspection of the data, the six groups were ordered along the radicalization continuum as follows: In Stage I were two groups, nonactivist lows and sympathizer lows. These groups represented the least radicalized, in terms of both behavioral and ideological commitment. In Stage II of the model were the dissident activist lows, nonactivist highs, and sympathetic highs—the three "intermediate" groups. Finally, there was the most radicalized group, the dissident activist highs. We have let this group stand by itself in Stage III because of its combination of endorsement of Revolutionary Tactics and previous participation in confrontation activities. Table 8.4 summarizes this information. The reader is urged to become familiar with this table as this classification scheme underlies the analyses in this chapter and the next one.

Stage I: Changes in Attitude toward the Status Quo. The importance of changes in traditional morality during Stage I of the process can be seen by comparing the attitudes of the individuals in the Stage I groups with those in groups at other stages. The means for the groups as freshmen on the five attitude scales are depicted in Figure 8.2. It shows that Stage I freshmen were clearly distinguished from freshmen in either of the other stages on the Traditional Moralism scale. Their scores were higher and barely overlapped with the rest of the sample ($t=6.35$, $df=119$, $p<.001$). This pattern was not true of the other scales. (Note

---

[2] The results from these procedures have been verified in subsequent analyses using covariance and cross-lag panel correlations. Comparisons of the mean responses among other of our samples assumed to be at different stages of radicalization provide further support.

Table 8.4
Distribution of the Six Attitude-Activity Groups
According to Radicalization Stage as Freshmen

Stage I	Stage II	Stage III
Nonactivist lows	Dissident activist lows	Dissident activist highs
Sympathizer lows	Nonactivist lows	
	Sympathizer highs	

that the students were divided into stages according to their score on Revolutionary Tactics, hence the large differences on this scale.)

Additional evidence for the significance of Traditional Moralism at this stage of radicalization comes from an analysis of change scores on this scale from freshman to sophomore year. If our hypothesis is correct, those freshmen who began in Stage I and increased their endorsement of Revolutionary Tactics during the year (i.e., became radicalized) should be the only respondents exhibiting a concomitant decrease in traditional morality. Table 8.5 presents the relevant data. A negative mean proportionate change score indicates a lessening in en-

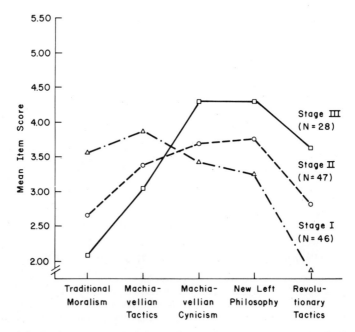

Figure 8.2. Freshman New Left scale scores of students at each stage of radicalization.

Table 8.5

Mean Proportionate Change Scores on the Traditional Moralism Scale from Freshman to Sophomore Year for Panel Sample Respondents in Each Stage of the Radicalization Process

	Stage I	Stage II	Stage III
Radicalized during freshman year[a]			
$\overline{X}$	−.17	−.10	−.10
SD	.30	.29	.20
N	22	24	9
Not radicalized during freshman year			
$\overline{X}$	−.02	−.14	+.04
SD	.18	.31	.21
N	24	23	11

[a]Each of the six attitude-activity groups were split at about the median of proportionate change on Revolutionary Tactics scores, to determine who in the group had been radicalized. Attempts were made to divide at natural breaks in the scores. Dissident activist highs were divided into three groups because of the distribution on their scores—one group whose Revolutionary Tactics scores increased, one group whose scores decreased, and a third group whose scores were unchanged. The data from the latter group are not presented in the table. See Chapter 9 for a more complete account.

dorsement of conventional values (the radicalized response); a positive score indicates an increase (the conservatized response). The students initially in Stage I *and* later radicalized decreased the most on Traditional Moralism of any of the groups, showing the only change significantly different from zero (t=2.61, df=21, p<.02).

These data suggest that attitudes toward traditional morality formed a major bridge between State I and Stage II of the radicalization process. Stage I individuals had significantly higher Traditional Moralism scores than those in Stages II and III. If individuals in Stage I moved toward the radical end of the continuum, they showed a significant decrease in their belief in conventional values, a decrease that was not exhibited by any other radicalized or nonradicalized group.

Stage II: Changes in New Left Philosophy and Machiavellian Cynicism. The relationship of changes in New Left Philosophy and Machiavellian Cynicism during the second stage can perhaps best be seen from a comparison of attitude scores among each of the groups in Stage II. First let us return to Figure 8.2 to examine the scores of the activist lows and nonactivist highs, two groups that might be considered "inconsistent" in their attitudes and behavior. The nonactivist highs are similar to the other Stage II groups (activist lows and sympathizer highs) on all scales but New Left Philosophy; there they cluster with the two Stage I groups. On the other hand, the activist lows differ substantially from their fellow stage-mates only on Machiavellian Cynicism (excluding, of course, Revolutionary Tactics, since they do so by definition).

In Table 8.6 the proportionate change scores on these two scales, comparing those who became radicalized with those who did not, are shown. Not surprisingly, those students who were classified as nonactivist highs when they entered college and were radicalized at Columbia show the largest increase in endorsement of New Left Philosophy. An analogous situation is true of the radicalized activist lows on Machiavellian Cynicism. These differences suggest a compensatory mechanism; in order to move to the next stage, individuals had to reach a certain level of endorsement of Machiavellian Cynicism and New Left Philosophy. For the nonactivist highs this meant a large increase in their scores on New Left Philosophy, since as freshmen they were near the conservative end of the scale; for activist lows it meant a similar increase in their initially low scores on Machiavellian Cynicism.

Stage II and III: Consistency between Attitude and Behavior.   When examining the background data for variables occurring concomitantly with an increase in endorsement of radical beliefs, our attention focused on change in behavior. Was a change in political attitudes associated with a simultaneous change in degree of participation in political activities? More specifically, would those students whose attitudes became more radical from freshman to sophomore year show a corresponding increase in participation in radical causes, and would those whose attitudes became less radical show a corresponding decrease?

In order to test this hypothesis, we first had to devise a new classification scheme for the activities reported by the students on the sophomore year questionnaire. Since, as sophomores, 81% of the panel fell into our original activist category and only 25% of those who had entered Columbia as sympathizers or nonactivists had *not* increased their activity to some extent, we used a five-category classification scheme which permitted a more finely discriminating measure of political involvement. An a apriori system was then devised that divided the panel into three parts—those whose behavior became more radical over the course of the year, those whose behavior stayed the same, and those whose behavior became less radical.[3]

Table 8.7 shows the mean belief change scores (proportionate change on Revolutionary Tactics) for the six attitude-activity groups at each of these three levels of behavior change. An analysis of variance revealed a significant main effect of behavior change supporting a consistency hypothesis ($F=13.75$, $df=2,113$,

[3] For a detailed description of the new categories and the scoring system, see Appendix D.

Table 8.6

Mean Proportionate Change Scores on the New Left Philosophy and Machiavellian Cynicism Scales from Freshman to Sophomore Year for the Three Attitude-Activity Groups of Stage II

	Dissident activist lows	Nonactivist highs	Sympathizer highs
New Left Philosophy			
Radicalized during Freshman year			
$\bar{X}$	.06	.22	.08
SD	.21	.21	.22
N	8	10	6
Not radicalized during freshman year			
$\bar{X}$	−.18	−.09	−.03
SD	.22	.21	.28
N	5	11	7
Machiavellian Cynicism			
Radicalized during freshman year			
$\bar{X}$	.15	.13	−.02
SD	.24	.16	.17
N	8	10	6
Not radicalized during freshman year			
$\bar{X}$	−.11	−.04	−.02
SD	.28	.22	.29
N	5	11	7

$p<.01$). The respondents whose involvement in radical political activities had increased were more likely to have increased their endorsement of revolutionary tactics; those whose involvement had lessened were likely to have decreased their endorsement. However, further inspection of the data indicated that this consistency was significant only for those respondents who, regardless of precollege activity, had initially (early freshman year) scored high on the Revolutionary Tactics scale. It was not significant for those who had scored low on that scale.[4]

---

[4] The data were analyzed in several other ways, but the results were always the same: consistency among the highs and not among the lows.

Table 8.7

Mean Proportionate Change Scores on the Revolutionary Tactics Scale from Freshman to Sophomore Year for the Six Attitude-Activity Groups, by Level of Behavior Change

	Activity change								
	Increase			No change			Decrease		
	N	$\bar{X}$	SD	N	$\bar{X}$	SD	N	$\bar{X}$	SD
Dissident activist highs	8	.32	.28	17	−.10	.19	3	−.15	.11
Sympathizer highs	4	.16	.40	8	−.02	.17	1	−.48	–
Nonactivist highs	9	.11	.23	4	−.07	.21	8	−.17	.24
Dissident activist lows	4	.26	.26	4	.18	.10	5	.23	.17
Sympathizer lows	4	.14	.08	7	.23	.15	9	−.02	.16
Nonactivist lows	8	.22	.20	8	.14	.12	10	.06	.07
All groups scoring high on Revolutionary Tactics scale	21	.20	.30	29	−.07	.19	12	−.19	.22
All groups scoring low on Revolutionary Tactics scale	16	.21	.20	19	.18	.13	24	.07	.16

Perhaps the best comparison groups in this regard are the activist highs and the nonactivist lows. Both arrived at Columbia with attitudes consistent with behavior. Therefore, any change in one of the variables over the year should have led to compensatory change in the other. (This would not necessarily be the case for groups such as the activist lows or nonactivist highs; they had come to Columbia in a state of inconsistency, which they could have reduced by change in either attitude or behavior.) While individuals in both groups showed trends toward consistency, that for the activist highs was significant (post hoc $F=6.86, p<.05$) and that for the nonactivist lows was not (post hoc $F<1$).

The striking consistency among the activist highs (Stage III) can be seen in Table 8.8, which presents the relationship between activity change and attitude change from freshman to sophomore year for the 28 activist highs. Seven of the eight individuals who increased their political participation (as measured by our

Table 8.8
Relationship between Attitude Change and Behavior Change from Freshman to Sophomore Year among the Activist Highs

Attitude change[a]	Activity change			
	Decrease	No change	Increase	Total
Increase	0	2	7	9
No change	0	7	1	8
Decrease	3	8	0	11
Totals	3	17	11	28

[a]As measured on the Revolutionary Tactics scale.

newly created categories) increased their scores on Revolutionary Tactics as well. The three whose participation decreased exhibited decreased scores on Revolutionary Tactics over the year.

Stage III: Interest in Tactical Questions. The radicals who became more radical while at Columbia reported in their sophomore year that they had also become more interested in tactical questions as opposed to questions pertaining to specific issues. The crucial issues having been already agreed upon—the Vietnam War, racism, and the "repressive" structure of society (see Table 8.9)—they now

Table 8.9
Percentage of Activist Highs That Reported Themselves Interested in Specific Issues as Sophomores[a]

	Vietnam War	Racism	Economy	Environment	Societal structure
Students whose endorsement of Revolutionary Tactics increased from freshman to sophomore year ($N=9$)	65	56	11	22	56
Students whose endorsement of Revolutionary Tactics decreased from freshman to sophomore year ($N=11$)	54	45	18	64	9

[a]The percentage that spontaneously cited the issue when asked to list issues in which they were interested. The table does not include the eight students whose scores on the Revolutionary Tactics scale did not change over the year.

debated the appropriate means to achieve their goals. At first, one might consider this finding to be an artifact of using change on the Revolutionary Tactics scale as the dependent measure. However, since none of the five other radicalized groups, all showing similar amounts of proportionate attitude change, reported an increasing interest in tactics, the argument seems moot.

Conversely, the activist highs, whose endorsement of Revolutionary Tactics decreased over the year, became more interested in issues as opposed to tactics. When they were asked to list the issues in which they were most interested, many spontaneously mentioned "the environment." Table 8.9 indicates that at a time when ecological concerns were not yet in vogue (fall 1969), 64% of this group expressed an interest in them while only 22% of the radicalized activist highs and 13% of the rest of the sample did so. Although the "deradicalized" activist highs may have deserted the ranks of the New Left vanguard, they seem to have joined the less radical sister movement, the "New Politics" of the early 1970s.

Discussion

The radicalization process, as we have described it, began with a lessening in endorsement of traditional values. Based on our knowledge about the nature of the New Left movement this change appears to be a logical first step.

The New Left movement arose during the early 1960s in response to what was felt to be an urgent need for political action to achieve social change. The initial focus of its attack was twofold—a resolution of racial inequities and an end to the United States Cold War foreign policy (Jacobs & Landau, 1966). Although the movement is now probably best described as a counterculture searching for new modes of living, it first and foremost represented a rejection of status quo attitudes and a willingness to accept new ideas. These beliefs were clearly illustrated by the following section of the Port Huron Statement, a document written at the founding convention of Students for a Democratic Society (SDS) in 1962:

> Some would have us believe that Americans feel contentment amidst prosperity— but might it not better be called a glaze above deeply felt anxieties about their role in the new world? And if these anxieties produce a developed indifference to human affairs, do they not as well produce a yearning to believe there *is* an alternative to the present, that something *can* be done to change circumstances in the school, the workplaces, the bureaucracies, the government? It is to this latter yearning, at once the spark and engine of change, that we direct our present appeal. The search for truly democratic alternatives to the present, and a commitment to social experimentation with them, is a worthy and fulfilling human enterprise, one which moves us and, we hope, others today [Jacobs & Landau, 1966, p. 152].

A rejection of items on the Traditional Moralism scale reflects much of this same spirit. The scale was not developed to measure underlying personality dynamics as was its forefather the *F*-scale, but rather to capture beliefs characterizing American middle-class society—law and order, the right to private property, and the value of tradition. When becoming part of a movement that is attempting to restructure society, it is appropriate that a rejection of these values should constitute the initial step in the conversion process.

The change in scores on Traditional Moralism was followed by a growing pessimism about life and the political system. The importance for radicalization of this cynical outlook cannot be overestimated. On the basis of an analysis of a cross-lag panel correlation, Bachman (1972) reported that loss of trust in the American government caused high school students to become opposed to the Vietnam War. Although anti-Vietnam attitudes probably constitute only a small part of what we have defined as radicalism, Bachman's data confirm the central role in the radicalization process of attitudes such as those measured by the Machiavellian Cynicism scale.

However, it is likely that the pessimism tapped by the Machiavellian Cynicism scale is crucial to changing ideas in both political directions, toward the right as well as toward the left. Alienation from one's fellowmen and dissatisfaction with existing or future government programs would both seem to be important catalysts to any fundamental switch in political viewpoint. The reason for the move toward the left rather than toward the right among the Columbia students in our sample may have been the coupling of this discontent with an endorsement of the ideas embodied in the New Left Philosophy scale. Many individuals believe that people are basically untrustworthy and weak—an attitude that is tapped by the Machiavellian Cynicism scale. Conservatives consider these to be inherent characteristics of man, an idea which necessarily leads to a desire for tighter controls on man's behavior. The Columbia radicals, however, as indicated by the New Left Philosophy scale, believe the present societal structure is responsible for the weakness of man. Men could be "brave" if the structure were altered. Thus, the radicals of the left concentrate their efforts on developing humanistic means, such as "participatory democracy," to bring men together into trusting relationships.

A major finding of the research presented in this chapter is that consistency between attitudes and behavior was observed among students who came to Columbia believing in the use of disruption for political aims (scores above the median on the Revolutionary Tactics scale) but not among students who did not endorse confrontation as a political tactic. We can only speculate as to the reasons for this difference. It is likely that attitude change among the low-scoring group (i.e., those freshmen who scored below the median on the Revolutionary Tactics scale) was essentially a socialization phenomenon. Almost all of them became radicalized during the period of the panel study, while only about one-half of the highs did (see Table 8.3). The lows' increased endorsement of New Left attitudes therefore may not have required a major adjustment in behavior, because most of their friends were experiencing a similar change. (Recall that friendships were highly related to political attitudes, see Chapter 7.) Highs, on the other hand, were probably more conscious of shifts in their attitudes. Since not all their friends were changing in the same direction, differences of opinion as a result of diverging attitudes could have been highly salient, and demanding of compensatory changes in behavior. It is also possible that once an individual had reached Stage II on the continuum, his attitudes became more important to him, thereby resulting in more perceived inconsistency and a need for resolution of that inconsistency (Festinger, 1957).

A broader issue raised by this analysis pertains to the causal direction of consistency between attitudes and behavior: Do attitudes play a more important role than behavior in causing subsequent attitude and behavior change, or does behavior play the more important role?

A careful examination of our data suggests that while both processes were probably operating, attitudes and not behavior had the most impact on the radicalization we observed. In the first place, as Table 8.2 indicated, initial attitude scores on the Revolutionary Tactics scale predicted subsequent radicalization, while precollege activity did not. The same point can be made about prediction of activity change. A check of the frequencies in each cell in Table 8.7 indicates that students who entered Columbia endorsing the use of disruptive tactics (i.e., high score on the Revolutionary Tactics scale) were less likely to decrease their involvement in political protest activity over the year than were those who came to college not endorsing revolutionary tactics. On the other hand, the latter, low group was relatively less likely to increase participation in protests (X^2=6.69, df=2, p<.05). Initial political activity levels bore little relationship to subsequent changes in activity (X^2=7.56, df=4, p>.10).

In the social psychological literature on consistency, little emphasis has been given to the effect of attitudes on behavior change. Instead, the research has focused on the opposite relationship—that behavior can cause changes in attitudes, a hypothesis developed from cognitive dissonance theory (Festinger, 1957). Hundreds (or perhaps thousands) of experiments, almost all in the laboratory, have been ingeniously devised to test the notion that if an individual chooses to perform an act inconsistent with his beliefs he will change his attitudes to be consistent with his behavior. We began our research with this hypothesis in mind, hence the reason for the importance we attached to the occurrence of major campus demonstrations during the year of panel study. However, we now feel that among our respondents an individual's attitudes played a more significant causal role in radicalization than did his behavior.

Inconsistency among attitudes or between attitudes and behavior can be resolved in different ways, of which attitude change is only one. Compartmentalization, denial, and rationalization are alternatives suggested by theorists, including Festinger (Festinger, 1957; Abelson, 1959). However, most studies of cognitive dissonance have created situations that have made means of resolving the inconsistency other than attitude change less likely.

In the "real world," where the controls of the experimenter are absent and many alternatives for reducing dissonance are available, it seems likely that resolution of inconsistent *behavior* would be especially subject to modes other than attitude change. Behavior, particularly political protest behavior on a radical college campus, could easily be rationalized and perceived as due to the constraining situational factors of friends, chance, and excitement, and not to one's own beliefs. Hence, political behavior may not be seen as inconsistent with other attitudes or behavior and therefore no need to change attitudes would result. A similar kind of interpretation can be derived from attribution theory. Jones and Nisbett (1971) suggest that an actor more often attributes his actions (i.e., his behavior) to the external constraints of the environment than to his own underlying personality or motivational traits. However, such an attribution process would not seem likely when an individual attempts to understand why he/she holds the particular attitude he/she does. Attitudes are personal, covert commitments, and if not expressed in a public forum, they may not be perceived as affected by social constraints to the same degree as actions (Warner & DeFleur, 1969). Persons may accept many of their attitudes as truly intrinsic to themselves and modify their behavior according to perceived inconsistencies.

Summary

A three-stage model of the radicalization process was proposed based on data collected from a panel sample of Columbia students during their freshman and sophomore years.

The first step toward radicalization appeared to be a lessening in commitment to the tenets of the status quo as measured by scores on the Traditional Moralism scale. At the next stage, scores on the New Left Philosophy scale and the Machiavellian Cynicism scale were found to be important. As individuals became radicalized they also increased their endorsement of New Left Philosophy and Machiavellian Cynicism, compensating for initially low scores on these scales. In addition, a trend toward consistency between changes in attitudes and changes in behavior was observed. In the final stage, interest in tactical questions as opposed to issues became paramount.

The significance of the findings in relation to political attitude change and to theories of cognitive consistency was discussed.

9
The
Radicalized Students

In the previous chapter we presented a model of the radicalization process, describing the changes in attitudes and behavior that occurred among students who increased their endorsement of Revolutionary Tactics. The present chapter examines the characteristics of students whose beliefs about the use of radical tactics shifted toward the left from the beginning of their freshman year to the beginning of their sophomore year and compares them to the characteristics of students whose beliefs did not shift to the left. In discussing this material we do not mean to imply strict causal relationships between the differentiating characteristics and radicalization. Such a relationship would be impossible to determine, given the correlational nature of the study. Rather, we conceive of the distinguishing variables as facilitating the change process, thereby increasing an individual's vulnerability to attitude change toward the left.

The analysis of data for this chapter, as for the preceding chapter, took several forms, all producing similar results. In order to maintain continuity with the radicalization process model, we have followed the same format, dividing the panel members into six groups according to their freshman scores on the Revolutionary Tactics scale and their precollege political activity. Proportionate change on the Revolutionary Tactics scale has again been used as the main dependent measure reflecting degree of radicalization. Since the analysis required identifying characteristics of students who became radicalized and of those who did not, a further subdivision of the sample based on individual proportionate change scores on the Revolutionary Tactics scale was made. Each of the six groups was divided in half on the basis of the distribution of change scores of its own group members. This procedure was chosen because we wanted to understand how the radicalization process affected students as a function of the particular political position held upon arrival at college. A median split of the entire sample would have resulted in highly unequal cell frequencies because almost all of the students initially scoring low on the Revolutionary Tactics scale showed some radicalization, while those scoring high did not (see Chapter 8).

Individuals with high proportionate change scores in relation to the other members of their group have been called "radicalized"; those with low, zero, or negative proportionate change scores have been called "nonradicalized" (cf. Tables 8.5 and 8.9). The mean changes for these 12 groups are presented in Table 9.1.

This chapter is divided into two sections. In the first section, variables that were related to radicalization, regardless of which of the six basic groups the individuals belonged to are described. This part involves a comparison of so-called radicalized students with those termed nonradicalized. The second section deals with characteristics that facilitate radicalization at each of the three stages of the radicalization process model. Radicalized respondents from each of the

Table 9.1
Comparison of Mean Proportionate Change Scores on the Revolutionary Tactics Scale for Radicalized and Nonradicalized Students

	Initial activity level					
	Nonactivists		Sympa-thizers		Dissident activists[a]	
	$\bar{X}$	SD	$\bar{X}$	SD	$\bar{X}$	SD
High initial score on Revolutionary Tactics scale						
Radicalized	+.20	.11	+.23	.28	+.32	.36
	(N=10)		(N=6)		(N=9)	
Nonradicalized	−.23	.13	−.19	.16	−.24	.11
	(N=11)		(N=7)		(N=11)	
Low initial score on Revolutionary Tactics scale						
Radicalized	+.24	.16	+.22	.12	+.34	.16
	(N=12)		(N=10)		(N=8)	
Nonradicalized	+.04	.05	−.02	.15	+.04	.03
	(N=14)		(N=10)		(N=5)	

[a]The group of eight activist highs who showed no change on the Revolutionary Tactics scale is not included.

six groups assumed to be at a particular stage of the model are compared with their nonradicalized counterparts. The clustering of the groups at stages is the same as that used to describe the radicalization process in Chapter 8 (cf. Table 8.4).

Characteristics Associated with Radicalization at All Stages

While there was variability in the kinds of interpersonal contacts a student had during his freshman year, the combination of living in New York City and attending Columbia College almost guaranteed that all members of the panel sample were exposed to some radical ideas in formal or informal discussion with other people during the year. Since interpersonal relationships have been found to be an important factor increasing the likelihood of attitude change (Lazarsfeld, Berelson, & Gaudet, 1968; Barton, 1972), we first addressed ourselves to the degree of correlation between such contacts and radicalization.

Incoming freshman panel members had been asked to list their sources of information about the Columbia demonstrations the previous spring. The responses were divided into two categories—those that involved personal observation or interpersonal contacts, such as discussions with friends, and those that involved only the media and were nonpersonal. As shown in Table 9.2, the students subsequently radicalized reported gathering their information from the sources included in the first category (i.e., own observation and talking to

Table 9.2

Frequency of Radicalization by Method of Gathering Information about 1968 Columbia Crisis[a]

	Method of gathering information		
	By interpersonal interaction and personal observation	Through the media	Total
Students who became radicalized	33	22	55
Students who did not become radicalized	22	36	58
Totals	55	58	113

[a]Does not include group of eight activist highs whose Revolutionary Tactics scores did not change over the course of the year.

others) more often than did those not radicalized. Students who were not radicalized more often relied on the media ($X^2 = 5.50$, $df=1$, $p<.025$).

Friendship patterns were also found to be related to radicalization. Each panel member circled the political positions of his close friends as well as himself on a 21-point conservative-radical scale. These data were analyzed in two ways: according to the number of scale points between a respondent's most radical and most conservative friend (i.e., the range of politics among his friends) and according to the number of scale points separating a respondent's self-rating and the average rating of his friends (i.e., the magnitude of the absolute discrepancy of friends from self). Table 9.3 presents the results. Individuals who became radicalized reported a significantly smaller range of positions for their friends than did those who did not become radicalized ($t = 2.54$, $df = 110$, $p <.05$). While there was no way of verifying the reported attitudes, the data indicate that the students who became more radical during their freshman year at Columbia at least *perceived* their friends as a politically homogeneous group. This lack of disparity of positions presumably means the respondent was confronted with fewer conflicting opinions, which may have made it easier for him to change as he did. In addition, as shown in Table 9.3, the radicalized students saw themselves as closer to their friends in political beliefs than did the nonradicalized. This finding did not reach significance by parametric tests. However, the radicalized students reported their own positions to be less discrepant from those of their friends than did the nonradicalized in five of the six initial activity-attitude

Table 9.3
Relationship between Radicalization and the Perceived Political Positions of Friends[a]

	Difference between most conservative and most radical friend		Absolute discrepancy between self-rating and average of judged positions of friends	
	$\bar{X}$	SD	$\bar{X}$	SD
Students who became radicalized (N=54)	4.81	4.96	2.11	1.98
Students who did not become radicalized (N=58)	7.34	5.56	2.58	2.42

[a]Does not include one student who did not respond to the relevant questions or group of eight activist highs whose Revolutionary Tactics scores did not change over the year. Political position rated on a 21-point conservative-radical scale.

groups ($p < .05$ by binomial test). In other words, the radicalized students appeared to be characterized by having a high degree of social support from friends; not only did they have homogeneous clusters of close friends, but the opinions of their friends were similar to their own.

However, the nature of the students' relationships with their parents were not related to radicalization. The panel members were asked to indicate degree of moral support given by both father and mother and to circle the political positions of each of their parents. No difference between radicalized and nonradicalized respondents on any of these four questions were found. Parents' political attitudes as determined by reports of the parents themselves (see Chapter 5) also did not differentiate those sons who were radicalized from those who were not.

From an analysis of socioeconomic status it appeared that the less affluent students were more likely to become radicalized than the more affluent ones. As sophomores, the members of the panel sample were asked: "Concerning your financial secruity now, would you say you feel (1) very secure, (2) fairly secure, or (3) not very secure." The results presented in Table 9.4 indicate that those students who reported being not very financially secure were significantly more likely to have been radicalized than those indicating relatively greater security ($X^2 = 6.72$, $df = 2$, $p < .05$). Before interpreting these data, we looked for some indication of the accuracy of the self-reports with respect to actual economic position. Although no direct measure of the variable, such as family income, was available, educational level of the respondents' fathers, another indicator of socioeconomic status, was known. This measure was found to relate significantly with the responses to the financial security question ($X^2 = 14.36$, $df = 4$, $p < .01$). The higher the educational level of the respondent's father, the more secure he felt.

Given the probable veridicality of the self-reports, it is tempting to consider the finding as supporting the Marxian belief in the ultimate revolution of the proletariat. However, the fact that the question was asked during sophomore year means that the responses were given retrospective to the student's radicalization, and thus it raises serious doubts as to whether such an interpretation is viable. It is possible that a student's perspective about his economic status was tempered by two factors. First, aware of his shift toward the left, he may have consciously or unconsciously distorted his report of his family's economic security to conform to the Marxian dialect. Considering the romantic idealism often attributed to members of the New Left (Newfield, 1966), such an explanation would not seem unrealistic. In the second place, the general affluence of most Columbia students must be acknowledged. Those from more modest, although not lower-class (i.e., "proletariat") backgrounds, may have felt financially deprived when they compared themselves to their schoolmates. In

Table 9.4
Degree of Self-Reported Present Financial Security by Radicalization[a]

	Very secure	Fairly secure	Not very secure	Total
Students who became radicalized	13	32	9	54
Students who did not become radicalized	25	30	3	58
Totals	38	62	12	112

[a]Does not include one student who did not respond to financial security question or group of eight activist highs whose Revolutionary Tactics scores did not change over the year.

this case, the data would not support a strict Marxian analysis; the radicalized would still primarily have come from the middle class, but their insecurity would be relative to the wealth immediately around them, rather than to that of the rest of society.

CHARACTERISTICS ASSOCIATED WITH RADICALIZATION AT EACH OF THE THREE STAGES OF THE PROCESS

We now turn to the analyses of the data according to the three stages of the radicalization model.

Conservative: Stage I. The preceding chapter suggested that movement from the first stage to the second stage of radicalization was characterized by an increasing rejection of traditional values as measured by the Traditional Moralism scale. These speculations were based on observed differences between the two conservative groups—nonactivist lows and sympathizer lows—and the rest of the sample. In this section we will compare the responses of those initially conservative students who later became radicalized to the responses of those within the same two groups who did not become radicalized.

It occurred to us that one likely characteristic differentiating students radicalized during college from those not radicalized would be their attitudes upon entering college; perhaps those who were radicalized initially held more left-wing beliefs. In order to determine whether this was indeed true, the freshman scores on all five attitudes scales were examined. For only one scale, Traditional Moralism, was the difference between radicalized and nonradicalized students significant. As shown in Table 9.5, upon arrival at Columbia conservative

Table 9.5

Means and Standard Deviations on Traditional Moralism Scale for Respondents in Stage I Groups as Freshmen

	Radicalized		Nonradicalized	
	$\bar{X}$	SD	$\bar{X}$	SD
Nonactivist lows	3.27	.76	4.02	.98
	(N=12)		(N=14)	
Sympathizer lows	3.16	.81	3.75	1.21
	(N=10)		(N=10)	
Totals	3.22	.77	3.91	1.07
	(N=22)		(N=24)	

students who later became more left-wing in their beliefs acknowledged less support for conventional values, i.e., lower scores on the Traditional Moralism scale, than did those students who did not become radicalized. It should be emphasized that this was the only scale on which a difference was found; both groups were equally low in their endorsement of radical beliefs on the other four scales. Of further note is the fact that scores on Traditional Moralism (or on any of the other scales) did not differentiate the radicalized from the nonradicalized among the moderate (Stage II) or radical (Stage III) groups.

There were other indicators of unwillingness on the part of radicalized students to accept the status quo. They were more likely to have belonged to organizations in high school that were interested in social amelioration (e.g., tutoring, philanthropic fund-raising) than were their nonradicalized peers. Their ideas about the purpose of college education also reflected dissatisfaction with traditional American values. During freshman orientation week they indicated on our questionnaire that they believed the university should be a place for "learning free from outside pressure," rather than a place for "training directly applicable to the careers of its students," the latter being the most common response of those who were not later radicalized. Thus, it appears that among the panel members who entered college with political attitudes to the right of their classmates and without much experience in political protest (i.e., at Stage I), those whose beliefs about contemporary American society showed relatively greater flexibility and desire for change were more influenced by politicizing forces than were those students who did not question the existing mores.

Moderate: Stage II. The strategy for analyzing the data for the moderate respondents (Stage II) was identical to that used for Stage I. Those students who became radicalized at Columbia differed from the students who did not become radicalized with respect to three characteristics. (1) They were more likely to come from families whose parents had *never* been involved in politics; (2) they were more likely to have grown up in smaller cities (e.g., Rochester rather than New York City), and (3) they were more likely to have grown up in southern or western portions of the United States. The responses to these three questions were positively correlated with one another; in combination they suggest the potential radicalizing effect of the lack of political sophistication. Freshmen who came to college with an inclination toward radical beliefs or behavior were likely to be radicalized if they had lived in politically sparse environments. Freshmen with identical beliefs and histories of political participation but who had been exposed to politics during high school because they lived in large cities or because they had politically aware parents were likely to be resistant to radicalizing influences at Columbia.

Radical: Stage III.   Characteristics relating to the nature of high school activities differentiated those dissident activist highs who were radicalized from those who were not. Of the 9 individuals who increased their endorsement of Revolutionary Tactics while at Columbia, 7 reported on their freshman orientation week questionnaires that they had participated in some sort of activity during high school that could have led to their probation or expulsion from school. These activities included organizing and participating in protests against school policy, using the school newspaper to voice opinions opposing those of the school administration, and editing and distributing underground newspapers. Only 3 of the 11 students who did not become radicalized indicated similar involvement. Even though both groups reported equivalent amounts of political and nonpolitical extracurricular activity, the students who later became radicalized had apparently taken more risks, perhaps indicating a greater sense of commitment to their cause.

Discussion

The importance of the relationship between social context and political attitudes was stressed earlier (see Chapter 7). This same theme has emerged again during the analysis of the radicalization process. The interpersonal relationships of those in the Columbia panel who became radicalized differed in several ways from those who did not. The radicalized sought information about political events from their friends more often than from the media (the nonradicalized depended more heavily on the media). They also perceived their friends as a homogeneous group holding attitudes close to their own. However, they were not different from their nonradicalized peers with respect to variables dealing with relations with parents, i.e., moral support from parents and political attitudes of parents. There are at least two interpretations which follow from these data. In the first place, they point to a more powerful orientation toward peers than toward parents. Second, they suggest a refinement of a previous statement (see Chapter 7), which noted that the characteristics of an individual's social context such as his friends, his religious preference, and his educational philosophy, had a greater impact on the development of left-wing beliefs than did background characteristics, such as socioeconomic status. It appears that only the nature of the immediate social context, the one in which daily interactions occur, may be critical. Contacts with college friends facilitated the radicalization process, while those with parents, obviously on a more intermittent basis, had little effect on attitude change.

These data raise another question concerning the nature of the social context. To what extent was the radicalization due to the ambience of the Columbia campus or to changes in the larger society? Support for the importance of both factors can be found in the data. The significant relationship observed between initial attitudes and subsequent radicalization suggests that Columbia itself was a powerful socializing agent (see Chapter 8). The students who entered college endorsing the use of Revolutionary Tactics changed less than those who were not as favorably disposed to using such tactics. This finding can be explained as a result of the initially more conservative respondents needing to take on the values of their newly acquired reference group—Columbia. The initially radical freshmen did not have to change; they were already in the campus mainstream. The variance in scores on the Revolutionary Tactics scale also decreased from freshman to sophomore year for the sample as a whole, again indicating a homogenizing of political views. The variance did not decrease, for example, for scores on the less politically oriented Machiavellian Tactics scale.

Interviews about friendship patterns conducted in the spring of freshman year with a subsample of the original 153-member Columbia sample were also revealing. When asked why they had changed their political beliefs during their year at college, interviewees most often cited reasons peculiar to being at Columbia—discussion with campus radicals, belonging to campus political groups, participating in the rallies, minor takeovers of buildings, and community political actions. One of the local New York students, while describing his changes, remarked on the differences between his college friends and his high school buddies living only a few miles away. Whenever he went home, he found that relationships with them were strained. He had little left in common with them after only 6 months of separation.

While the radicalizing forces of the Columbia campus itself appear to be particularly potent, the importance of the larger society cannot be ignored. The general mood of the country's youth changed during the 1968-1969 academic year (Yankelovich, 1972; Bachman, 1972). The failure to find differences in attitudes between freshmen and upperclassmen for almost all of the samples gathered by us as well as in the Yankelovich-CBS survey attests to the impact of the national context. If socialization into a particular campus surround was the only factor operating, freshmen should have held different views than those of the upperclassmen. Panel members spontaneously reported on questionnaires that events such as Nixon's 1968 election and the publicity about the My Lai massacre were critical in changing their political beliefs toward the left. In short, both environments—the national and the immediate—were responsible for radicalization; unfortunately the relative importance of each cannot be assessed from the present data.

The relationship of scores on the Traditional Moralism scale to radicalization has been discussed in both this chapter and the previous one. Here we noted that radicalization was more likely among initially conservative students if they arrived at Columbia somewhat skeptical of the desirability of conventional values (i.e., relatively low scores on the Traditional Moralism scale). In Chapter 8, the first stage of the radicalization process was shown to involve a lessening of belief in conventional values (i.e., a decrease in scores on the Traditional Moralism scale). In this light, the low Traditional Moralism scores of the conservative students who were subsequently radicalized suggests an anticipatory socialization phenomenon. Although these radicalized students did not at the time they began college show any indication of radicalism, as measured by the Revolutionary Tactics scale, they may have prepared themselves to move in that direction by being less supportive of status quo values. This preparatory change might have been seen if precollege attitudes had been assessed. In any case, the evidence points to the fact that Traditional Moralism is a set of core attitudes that forms the foundation of radicalization.

A combination of variables relating to home town and parents' political life differentiated the radicalized from the nonradicalized among moderate (Stage II) respondents. This finding was unexpected. Given the traditional stereotype of the radical, the reverse might have been predicted, namely that students from urban, politically active families would be more easily radicalized. However, upon further consideration, the results seem reasonable. Students who grew up in less cosmopolitan areas probably had not engaged in political dialogue with family and community members because they were far removed from significant political events, especially those of a left-wing nature. Their beliefs, therefore, may not have been well formulated. The dearth of political argumentation meant that their ideas were seldom attacked and thus seldom had to be defended, and the possible flaws in their reasoning were presumably not recognized. Such a situation could render those students who were leaning toward a left-wing position vulnerable to the persuasion of the radicals, who constituted a large and vocal segment of the Columbia campus. On the other hand, students from urban environments or politically active families were undoubtedly more politically sophisticated and better able to formulate and articulate their views.

Their beliefs were a result of listening to many different opinions expressed by friends and the media or gleaned from first-hand experience with protests (which were more likely to be held in large than small cities). These individuals were thus better able to resist the seemingly convincing arguments of the radicalizing elements at Columbia than were those who had never undergone such experiences.

This interpretation of the data closely resembles McGuire's analogy between medical inoculations and propagandizing (McGuire, 1964). Vaccines contain small doses of disease-producing viruses, which help individuals resist the effects of later exposure to such diseases. Arguments involving beliefs or attitudes should act similarly. By exposing a person to opposing opinions and forcing him/her to defend his viewpoint, they should make him/her more capable of resisting subsequent propaganda. If our finding is indeed an illustration of inoculation theory, it would suggest that the variables we have isolated as differentiating the radicalized from the nonradicalized would differentiate individuals whose attitudes change in either direction, to the left or to the right.

Summary

This chapter compared the characteristics of students who became radicalized during their freshman year at Columbia with those of students who did not become radicalized during that time. The data examined were from a panel sample of Columbia students followed from the beginning of their freshman year to the beginning of their sophomore year. The students were divided into two groups—those who became relatively more left-wing in their beliefs about the use of radical tactics for political change and those who did not. Two analyses were performed; one examined characteristics of radicalized and nonradicalized students regardless of their political positions upon entering college, the other examined differential characteristics based on the political viewpoints that the students held upon their arrival at college.

Students who became radicalized had obtained information about campus political events (i.e., the 1968 Columbia crisis) through personal and interpersonal means, while those who were not later radicalized had relied on the media. The friends of radicalized students shared beliefs that were more homogeneous and closer to the students' own positions than did the nonradicalized. From the second analysis we found that students who came to Columbia relatively conservative in their beliefs and activities but who later became radicalized entered college with lower scores on the Traditional Moralism scale, a more "liberal" educational philosophy, and with more high school experience of working in extracurricular activities that involved community concerns, such as tutoring and philanthropy, than did the conservative students who were not subsequently radicalized. The initially moderate students who became radicalized were more often from less cosmopolitan areas, from families whose parents had not been politically active, and from the southern and midwestern regions of the country as compared with those who did not become radicalized. Radical freshmen students who became more radical during freshman year differed from their nonradicalized counterparts by having participated in activities during high school that could have led to their being suspended or expelled from high school. The findings suggested several processes that might have facilitated radicalization: the mediation of attitudes by the individual's immediate social context, anticipatory socialization, and resistance to attitude change through prior "inoculation."

10

Concluding Remarks

When the Columbia campus exploded in the spring of 1968 we were surprised; but we were not alone in our surprise. With the exception of David Truman (then Dean of Columbia College and heir-apparent to the presidency of the University), who several months before had publicly predicted campus rebellions if the Vietnam War continued, almost no one we knew had anticipated that colleges and universities would be the main targets for protest against the war. We soon became puzzled by what we witnessed. In the first place, journalistic accounts of the spring crisis contradicted or omitted many events we ourselves had witnessed. We also found some of the interpretations that both students and administrators gave to the events oversimplified. Most of the administrators we knew did not fit the radical definition of them as "lackeys of a fascistic America," and most of the student protesters we knew did not fit the role ascribed to them of young Brownshirts, spoiled brats, mentally disturbed freak-outs, or participants in an updated and politicized version of such fads of the past as pantie raids or goldfish gulping.

Perhaps predictably, our response to the chaos was to begin research. Since we were not convinced that the protesters were ideologically confused, as many commentators had contended, we set out to discover if there were patterns of values that distinguished them from their less involved peers. The "protester's profile" was developed and did indeed make appropriate discriminations. In an attempt to discover antecedents of New Left activism among college students we examined the social and familial background of both radical and more conservative students. Our results indicated little support for an "inheritance" model, in which children take on the attitudes of their family, or a "rebellion" model, in which radicals were mirror images of conservative parents. We found acceptance of some values and nonacceptance of others, but relationships to parents appeared to be less important correlates of radical ideology than was participation in youth counterculture. Finally, in studying the process of radicalization over a year at Columbia, it was possible to identify in a post hoc manner individual predispositions and situational factors that may have retarded or speeded up the radicalization process.

Before discussing the three major themes emerging from the data, it is important to review briefly our interpretation of the social context in which they emerged.

The Escalating Student Protest of the 1960s

It is rare that a chronological decade dovetails so nicely with a social movement as did the 1960s with the rise of student protest. Three events occurred in 1960 that were precursors of the New Left. On February 1, four black students in Greensboro, North Carolina ordered coffee at a previously whites-only lunch counter. This early confrontation captured the imagination of the idealistic young and led to an escalating series of sit-ins, marches, and other protests against the racial status quo. On June 17-19, the first national convention of an obscure group called Students for a Democratic Society was held in New York City, marking the emergence of the organization that came to play a prominent role in the protests of the 1960s. In November, John F. Kennedy was elected president, symbolizing to young college liberals a national swing toward youthful optimism after the doldrums of the 1950s. When, later in the 1960s, the flickering pictures on the television screens were of the assassinations of idolized political leaders and of atrocities in Vietnam, a wave of disenchantment with the established order began. Students prepared to question and challenge an established order that they viewed as hypocritical, and SDS and other radical groups prepared answers that had an increasing cogency among the politically involved.

By early 1968, the more idealistic and socially concerned students were strongly alienated from the Establishment. Two events were crucial in the channeling of disenchantment to action among college students. The first was the Tet offensive which, whatever its military effectiveness, was viewed on many campuses as confirming the lies they had been told about the successes of American forces in Vietnam. But, in our opinion, an even more basic cause was the announcement in the early spring of 1968 that draft deferments for graduate students were to be ended at the end of the semester. For many students, this brought the war home in a way that was intensely personal. Suddenly, escape from the draft was sealed off, and the prospect of service in a war for which there was little enthusiasm and a great deal of repulsion was a real possibility.

As was true of most college confrontations, there were a series of idiosyncratic events that sparked the Columbia revolt in late April of 1968. Black and white students attending a small rally to protest Columbia's indifference to the problems of the local Harlem community were rebuffed by police when they tried to take over the construction site of a new gym that Columbia had started in Morningside Park, a no-man's-land between the university campus and Harlem. The students then marched back to campus and occupied Hamilton Hall, which contained the undergraduate dean's office, and briefly held the dean hostage. Soon the blacks, mistrustful of white radicals, asked them to leave. It was night, and the dispossessed whites decided to go to Low Library, the central administration building. There was only an elderly campus guard at the door; they brushed him aside and entered the building. As police arrived, the occupiers scurried out by the windows. However, the mission of the police was only to remove a Rembrandt in the office of the president to protect it from damage. Their mission accomplished, the police departed with the picture, and the dissidents scrambled back in again. Subsequently, three other buildings were occupied by perhaps a thousand other students and sympathizers. It should be noted that the initial incident, the march on the gym site, was not too different from a number of previous rallies, all of which had attracted only a handful of protesters. A series of accidental happenings, abetted by administrative ineptitude, led to the escalation of the protest into a major confrontation that closed down the university; but students other than the hard core of radicals probably would not have participated in it had there not been widespread dissatisfaction about the Vietnam War.

The summer of 1968 saw the struggles between police and dissidents at the Democratic national convention and the emergence of two presidential candidates both of whom were "hard-liners" on Vietnam and detested and distrusted by activist college students. The wave of protest spread quickly to many college campuses.

It was within this period of escalating campus protest (1968-1970) that our data were collected. We started by gathering data on Columbia students. Surprised and intrigued by many of our findings, we were spurred to gather material on other samples, college and noncollege.

We now turn to the major conclusions of the research effort and our reflections upon them.

Reflections on the Protester's Profile

It has been alleged that most generals prepare for the next war on the assumption that it will be fought like the last one, despite intervening social and technological changes.

A similar pattern apparently occurred among older commentators with regard to the emergence of the New Left. Old leftists thought of it as a resurgence of traditional Marxist protest and were baffled because the New Left had no "ideology," such as plans for the millennium once the revolution was successful. Old conservatives also thought of it as a resurgence of the leftist protest of the 1930s and were convinced that the movement was inspired and financed by Moscow. In the same vein, social scientists tended to view the protest movement in terms of variables with which they were most familiar. Psychologists gave scales measuring masculinity-femininity, psychological adjustment, moral development, and so forth, to contrasting groups of radical and conservative students [Keniston (1973) prepared an extensive bibliography]. Sociologists compared notes and heatedly argued whether or not student rebellion was related to institutional size and consequent depersonalization of students in "knowledge factories." (One of the popular buttons of the time carried the message associated with IBM cards, "I'm a Human Being. Please do not fold, spindle, or mutilate.") Other analyses were made of the customary relationships between family demographic characteristics and student protest behavior (Greenstein, 1975, summarizes these studies).

Although these studies reported provocative and statistically significant findings, they were unable to explain satisfactorily, either in a statistical or in an intuitive sense, the differences in ideology between protesting and nonprotesting students. In an attempt to fill this void, we developed a pool of 90 items from which we created the five scales used in analyzing the protester's profile.

The pattern of scores that we found for Traditional Moralism, New Left Philosophy, and Revolutionary Tactics—three of the five scales used in the protester's profile—were easy to interpret. Dissidents, by definition, are low in agreement with the middle-American moralism that extols conventionality and the acceptance of recognized authority, hence their low Traditional Moralism scores. And in the late 1960s and early 1970s, dissent among the young came primarily from the New Left movement, whose ideology reflected a Rousseauean view of the goodness of natural man, a distrust of contemporary social institutions, and an espousal of tactics of confrontation and no compromise.

What was not clear initially were the implications of the split in Machiavellianism scores, the protesters scoring lower in Machiavellian tactics (i.e., rejecting the use of deceit, stressing the importance of honesty) and higher in cynicism about others, especially those in authority positions, as compared to their more conforming peers' scores. But with hindsight we now think that this split between honesty in interpersonal relationships and distrust of others is probably related, among other things, to a strong feeling of identification with peers (hence the desire to be candid) and of alienation from the older generation (seen as the generalized "others"). Such an interpretation of the results makes understandable a number of phenomena that have puzzled some observers. For example, a common observation of administrators and older professors (at Columbia, at least) was the difference between one-to-one interactions with the young and interactions with them en masse. Individually, the student's idealism, concern, and frankness were apparent. Yet the same person, when a member of a group confronting the authorities, played the role of intransigent rebel, casting the older persons in the role of defenders of a corrupt establishment.

Another implication of the dichotomy between their attitudes toward members of their peer group (with whom one could be open) and toward older members of society concerns the ease with which groups of dissidents could be infiltrated by young informers working for the government. Members of the "Gainesville 8" illustrate the point neatly. These eight men were accused of a bizarre plot to disrupt the Republican National Convention in 1972. The old house that served as their headquarters was protected by strong lights flooding the outside at night in order to aid the spotting of intruders; they had a large bulletin board covered with photographs and suspected government agents; and during the start of their trial they photographed embarkees from planes at the airport as a possible aid in identifying additional FBI operatives. Despite these precautions, which were not as paranoid as they sound (the "Gainesville 8" were continually hassled by federal, state, and local investigative officers), the group was remarkably un-suspecting of younger persons posing as fellow dissidents. Two of the defendants were startled when paid FBI informers at the trial turned out to be young men whom they had regarded as their best friends and confidants. If the young dissidents had endorsed the use of Machiavellian Tactics instead of rejecting their use, such events might not have occurred. The dissidents should have not only believed in distrusting anyone over 30, but also added the further admonition, "Be especially suspicious of anyone under 30." These speculations are consistent with a long line of social psychological research which indicates that persons with an empathetic view of others (low on Machiavellian tactics) underestimate the perfidy of others in interpersonal situations (Geis & Christie 1970).

An additional point can be made about the failure of the young dissidents to organize an effective political apparatus. Their *weltanshauung,* with its idealized view of man and distrust of authority, led to an abhorrence of formal organiza-tion, which, to quote from one of the New Left scale items, tended "to stifle the creativity of [group] members." This lack of organization, coupled with an absence of long-range political plans, suggests why the movement failed to sustain enough involvement to lead to effective political change.

In short, we would argue that the ideology of the New Left as reflected in the protester's profile foredoomed its failure as a viable political movement, even under the most favorable of circumstances.

The Peer Group and the Generation Gap

One of our initial problems was acceptance of the fact that traditional indicators of social background, such as parents' education, occupation, and so forth, had little or no relationship to student ideology. It gradually became apparent to us that our implicit model of political socialization might not apply to the generation of students who arrived at college in the late·1960s. Originally we had assumed that as children grew up they would absorb the value orientations of their families and that these would be reinforced by extrafamilial institutions that tended to be congruent with parental values. When children went to college they would be exposed to values differing from those of their parents, and during the college years would develop individual value systems that reflected a blend of earlier and newer influences. Individual resolutions of value conflicts might vary—from clinging tenaciously to parental values while rejecting noncompatible ideologies, to eschewing family values and embracing new ideologies—but the majority of resolutions would fall somewhere between the two extremes. According to this view, most people would have developed a general political ideology as young adults, which would influence their choice of roles within society. The latter would then tend to support a given individual's value system, thereby producing relative consistency through the rest of his/her adult life.

There were data, however, that cast doubt upon the validity of this model. First, upon arrival at Columbia, students were found to be significantly less conservative than their parents, which indicated that political socialization outside the family had occurred while students were still living at home and before exposure to college. Second, many of these values appeared well-established prior to college. There was no significant overall shift on four of the five scales during the first year of college. The one on which there was a significant increase, the endorsement of revolutionary tactics, related more to the implementation of the ideology of protest than to a shift in political orientation. Finally, there was little correlation between parental and student values when son-parent pairs were examined individually.

An explanation consistent with these data involves speculation about the historical context in which this generation was reared, as contrasted to that of their parents. There are three factors characteristic of the late 1940s and early 1950s that might have had an impact on the pattern of socialization of children born in this period. These are the post-World War II baby boom, the exodus of middle-class families from the cities to the suburbs, and the advent of television.

Following World War II, an unprecedented number of children were born within a limited time period. The high birthrate was coupled with migration to the suburbs and an increased emphasis on family life. Extensive housing tracts with families of comparable economic status and children of the same ages emerged as a new social phenomenon. In addition, the relative affluence of the postwar years afforded parents an opportunity to rear their families with more economic security than they had known when children themselves. An institution that expanded as a result of this new affluence was the nursery school, which provided an opportunity for early peer socialization in addition to that of the neighborhood.

The college generation of the late 1960s was characterized not only by early and extensive exposure to and interaction with peers, but also by being the first generation exposed to television from infancy. The numbers of children and the affluence of their parents did not escape the attention of Madison Avenue. Small children watched television programs that were sponsored by a massive industry devoted to promoting new products, many of them created especially for children. By the time they reached college in the late 1960s these young people had probably spent a larger portion of their lives in peer activities than had any earlier generation, with much of the content of these activities revolving around shared stimuli from the mass media. Thus, the locus of socialization was no longer primarily intrafamilial, as had been true of previous generations, but was instead primarily extrafamilial, dependent on both peers, and the electronic media (Mead, 1970).

The advent of television affected this generation in another way. Through it, the more malevolent aspects of American society became part of everyday life, and young people realized the sharp contrast between these and the benign images touted by public school teachers and textbooks. It is not surprising that this realization provoked strong feelings that the older generation had been hypocritical in preaching one thing and practicing another.

With these hindsights, we began to accept the pervasiveness of the generation gap in values highlighted by the research findings. Most intriguing was the direct comparison of father-son scores on Revolutionary Tactics. The overall nonsignificant correlation between the two scales masked the systematic tendency for sons of conservative fathers to be more radical than would have been predicted by regression equations. Similarly, the sons of radical fathers were less radical than would have been predicted. It was as if, within the broad rebellion against parental values that divided the generations, there were mini-rebellions against the positions of individual parents. In our interviews with the students, however, the difference in values was almost never described in such specific terms. The most common response was that the gap in values was so large that meaningful communication was nearly impossible.

Individual Change on a Radical Campus

One of the most striking results from the analysis of the panel data was that the changes that occurred between freshman and sophomore year (fall 1968 to fall 1969) were not philosophical but tactical. First, there was a significant mean increase only on the Revolutionary Tactics scale, a shift of about one-half of the standard deviation. Second, while endorsement of beliefs on the New Left Philosophy scale did not change, participation in protest activity increased dramatically. This theme was also elaborated during personal interviews with sample members. The same philosophical issues appear to concern both those students who were radicalized and those who were not. These two groups differed, however, in their views about the effectiveness of violence as a means to alleviate injustice. The radicalized saw violence as a potentially useful tactic. The nonradicalized saw it as a dangerous and antihumanistic tool.

The extent to which this finding can be generalized to other college campuses is questionable. Our analysis of the radicalization process suggests that attitudinal shifts away from conventional values and toward a more radical ideology probably precede, to some extent, shifts toward belief in the use of violent tactics to achieve social change, The members of our panel samples were fairly radical upon arrival at college—at least in comparison to the other samples we tested. This philosophical position, coupled with the diversity of radical organizations on the Columbia campus and the accessibility of protest demonstrations to Columbia students may have made the nature of their change relatively atypical. Students at other, less radical campuses, with fewer opportunities for protest, very likely did not show the same readiness to increase their endorsement of the use of violence. They probably reacted to the events of 1968-1969 by changing their beliefs toward a more radical philosophical position.

The panel analysis also suggested that the significant increase in endorsement of the items on the Revolutionary Tactics scale represented a socialization process into the mainstream ideology at Columbia. Degree of change on the scale was negatively correlated with freshman scale scores; that is, in general, the freshmen who held conservative attitudes were more likely to become more radical than were freshmen who already positively valued the use of violent tactics. In other words, most students in the panel sample seem to have accepted the Columbia campus, and its concomitant radical atmosphere, as a positive reference group for themselves. But what of those students for whom Columbia did not become a positive reference group? These were the students who entered Columbia with fairly conservative attitudes and were not radicalized. Our analysis points to two variables that may have affected this minority, both of which have implications for further research on social movements.

On the one hand, the fairly conservative students who were not radicalized began college with higher scores on the Traditional Moralism scale than did students who were radicalized, and this was the only scale on which they differed from their radicalized peers. The scores of the nonradicalized clustered at the top of the Traditional Moralism scale, while the scores of the radicalized, although lower, were spread over the length of the scale. Such a pattern suggests that the nonradicalized students were clinging to values that most of their classmates had already partially rejected.

What were these values to which they were clinging? Two pieces of data may help answer this question. Recall, first, that we found Traditional Moralism to be the scale that produced the highest and most consistent correlations between parents' and sons' scores. We also asked panel members to estimate the political positions of their parents on a 20-point scale (conservative to radical). When these estimates were correlated with parents' actual scores on the five scales, Traditional Moralism was the only scale for which there was a significant correlation. In other words, in the eyes of their sons, the parents' political beliefs were associated with beliefs in traditional moralism and not with the ideas underlying New Left Philosophy or Revolutionary Tactics, the two scales most closely identified with the New Left.

These correlations suggest that the Traditional Moralism scale taps basic societal values of the older generation that have been passed on to their children through the socialization process. The New Left movement, however, represented different values from those of the older generation. An activist member of the panel sample described it in the following way. "The movement's life style . . . is a kind of spontaneity, a kind of flexibility of having less of a stake in the world as it exists and thus being more able to accept change and work for change." The high scores on Traditional Moralism of students who were not radicalized indicate that they were not willing to reject these basic values of their parents, and, therefore, that they resisted the revolutionary fervor that captured their classmates. In fact, it is highly likely that scores on the Traditional Moralism scale would be a good predictor of attitude change within other counterculture movements.

The other variable that retarded radicalization among the more conservative panel members was prior political sophistication, associated with a highly cosmopolitan hometown and politically active parents. Students coming from small towns, who had little exposure to the rhetoric of the New Left or to political activity, had probably never argued against the barrage of new ideas that bombarded them upon arrival at Columbia. A few students described themselves as being swept along with the mainstream of the campus, powerless to stop the process. The more cosmopolitan students in the group, however, being already somewhat familiar with the ideas of the New Left could counter-argue them and consequently were less likely to be radicalized at Columbia than students who had no previous contact with radical ideas.

This line of reasoning has implications for understanding why the New Left movement lost its momentum. It suggests that one of the tactics of the movement—exposure through the media—may have contributed to its problems in attracting substantial recruits after 1970. The public had gradually become familiar with the ideas of the New Left, and with that familiarity came the ability to counterargue. No longer was there a situation, similar to the one at Columbia in 1968-1969, in which large numbers of people relatively unexposed to New Left beliefs could suddenly be thrust into an environment dominated by radicals. The New Left also thrived on intense emotional reaction by its supporters to events that they saw as examples of glaring injustice and flagrant misuse of power by the Establishment. By 1971 it is likely that, while most students accepted many of the ideas and rhetoric of the movement, the constant media exposure had dulled their reactions. No longer could an event provoke the same emotion or create the same enthusiasm for protest as did, for example, Nixon's decision to bomb Cambodia in 1970.

Epilogue

The campuses are quiet now, and, according to many observers of the college scene, students have reimmersed themselves in intellectual pursuits in a way that is reminiscent of the days prior to the civil rights and peace movements of the middle and late 1960s. This situation is a far cry from the heyday of demonstrations and strikes that caused the American public to believe that college protest was the major problem affecting the country (Gallup, May 1970).

There were many contributing factors to the demise of the New Left as a political movement after 1970. The phasing out of the draft removed some of the personal reasons for engaging in protest; the seemingly mindless violence of the Weathermen and other small but highly publicized groups of extremists appalled many of the student generation, as well as many older citizens; the infiltration and subversion of protest groups by government agents made the groups less effective; and the Nixon administration's policy of harrassing prominent antiwar leaders by putting them on trial for criminal conspiracy effectively tied up the symbolic leaders of the New Left in protracted legal hassles.

From our point of view the virtual absence of protest activity in the last few years poses an interesting research question. In 1968 we found a high correlation between the endorsement of statements reflecting what we have called Revolutionary Tactics and engagement in such behaviors as peace marches, sit-ins, picketing, and other overt manifestations of the disillusionment of the college generation with the course of political events. Furthermore, over the following year (1968-1969), students tended to change their political behavior and attitudes in a consistent manner; if they increased their endorsement of Revolutionary Tactics, they also increased their involvement in political activities in which these tactics were employed, and if they became less favorable toward using these types of tactics, they also decreased their involvement. The question now is: What happened to the underlying ideology when the behaviors reflecting it ceased? Although our emphasis in this book has been on the genesis and development of the New Left ideology, and not on the fate of the New Left movement, we offer some observations relating to whether the diminution of mass radical activity in the 1970s has had any effect upon the profound disenchantment with the established order characteristic of college students in the late 1960s.

In spring of 1974, a follow-up questionnaire was mailed to members of the Columbia College panel sample (class of 1972) whose addresses were on file with the alumni office at Columbia. At the present time, we can report only a preliminary analysis of the data. Of the 122 panel members, 75 returned questionnaires.[1] With regard to their scores on the New Left scales, there are two intriguing bits of data. First, attitude scores on the Machiavellian Tactics and Traditional Moralism scales dropped significantly (i.e., changed in a radical direction over the 5-year period). Second, on the two scales that most heavily reflected the left-wing politics of the late 1960s—New Left Philosophy and Revolutionary Tactics—scores remained virtually identical to sophomore levels. This means that with regard to Revolutionary Tactics, scores in 1974 were significantly more radical than they were 6 years earlier—freshman year in college. Such a finding is most surprising when one considers the content of the items on these two scales, content largely couched in the barricade jargon prevalent at the height of the New Left movement. Yet these Columbia alumni apparently still endorse statements dealing with the "Establishment" and a "mass revolutionary" party to the same extent as they did while sophomores in college.

Having to cope with the "real world" for 2 years following graduation has not caused the class of 1972 to become more conservative in their political beliefs. But what about their involvement in political activity? On the follow-up questionnaire we asked respondents to describe their political activity since graduation in June 1972. As noted earlier, we assumed that the sample members would have little to report, given the wane of the New Left movement. However, this was not the case. Only 19 of the 75 respondents (25%) indicated no political involvement—no petitions signed, no money contributed, no participation in protest demonstrations. On the other hand, 35 respondents (45% of the respondents) reported either participating in demonstrations or working for social and political organizations *since* graduation. Their activities included impeachment demonstrations, rallies in support of Russian Jewry, involvement in environmental groups, work for the McGovern presidential campaign, as well as participation in such local issues as low-cost housing and community medical service. We, unfortunately, have no nationwide data for the period 1972-1974 with which to compare these figures; but these data, coupled with the results from the New Left scales, suggest that these Columbia graduates have not become apolitical.

[1] While the freshman- and sophomore-year attitude scores of returnees were slightly more conservative than those of nonreturnees, the pattern of change of the scores during those 2 years was identical. Returnees showed the same significant increase on the Revolutionary Tactics scale described in previous chapters, and the same nonsignificant changes on the other scales; these, too, were in the same direction as nonreturnees. The evidence, therefore, suggests that the individuals in the follow-up analysis are indeed representative of the larger sample.

Further evidence for the continued presence of radical ideological commitment comes from data reported by Yankelovich (press releases, May 21, 1974). From a survey he conducted on a cross-sectional sample of college students in 1973 we were able to pick out items from the New Left scale that had been used in his 1969 sample, to which we have alluded in earlier chapters. The comparison of responses between the 1969 and 1973 surveys gives no indication of a shift in the conservative direction. If anything, the data indicate a slight shift toward a more radical philosophy.

Other data presented by Yankelovich indicate that, in fact, New Left values may have spread further, to members of the younger generation who had not previously been affected by the movement. We earlier noted that prior to 1968 the most rebellious segment of American youth came predominantly from families in which the parents were more likely to be better educated, have higher social status, and be politically more liberal. We found no such differences among Columbia students in 1968, and our analysis of data from the Yankelovich-CBS 1969 national survey indicated that it no longer held true for college students in general. Yankelovich's 1973 sample included noncollege respondents of the same age as students, and he noted, "Noncollege youth today are just about where the college population was in 1969 in adopting new social values and a new moral outlook." This suggests that just as blue jeans and beards spread from the scoffed-at radicals of the 1960s to other segments of the youth culture, so did the spirit of dissent. Diffusion of dissident ideology thus spread throughout the age cohort and, in doing so, crossed class, religious, and other boundaries demarcating segments of American society.

At this point one cannot help but wonder to what extent this spirit of dissent has diffused upward across age cohorts, especially to parents of college students of the past decade. One parent of a Columbia College sample member wrote us during the Senate Watergate hearings, "Current revelations of illegal, unethical, national political and governmental activities reminded me of your study. I see indications of a convergence of opinion between the generations." Such a change is, of course, a possibility, but we know of no data to support it.

What is indicated from this epilogue is that there are probably large numbers of college students and recent graduates who are alienated from the institutions of American society, and that this feeling has spread to less-educated members of the younger generation. The tides of discontent that rose in the late 1960s have not ebbed. The spirit of rebellious unrest may be dormant, but it has not yet passed away.

Appendix A

Stereotyped Appearance and Its Effect on Evaluation of the Draft Resister

RICHARD L. ZWEIGENHAFT

University of California, Santa Cruz

Many college students journeyed to New Hampshire in March 1968 to campaign for "peace candidate" Eugene McCarthy in the Democratic primary for President of the United States. Among them were a large number of bearded and long-haired males, who, upon arrival, were asked either to shave their beards and cut their hair or be prepared to work in a back room, out of the sight of New Hampshire voters. "Be neat and clean for Gene" became the well-publicized slogan of the young McCarthy canvassers, the assumption being that they would be more successful in their goal of political persuasion if they were neat and clean than if they were unkempt and dirty. The results in New Hampshire were more favorable to McCarthy than most had predicted, but the specific effect on the canvassers being "neat and clean" was never known.

There was an event of even greater significance to the nation's college campuses that occurred about a month prior to the New Hampshire primary. On February 19, 1968, General Hershey, Director of Selective Service, announced that all graduate school deferments would be canceled beginning September of that year. Seniors could no longer avoid the draft by continuing their education beyond college; once they graduated they would almost certainly be drafted. For many, the weeks that followed were filled with agonized soul-searching and constant reevaluation of the direction in which to proceed. Those who opposed the Vietnam War were forced to consider draft resistance as a real alternative, and the topic was much discussed at Columbia, as on campuses throughout the country.

The purpose of this study was to investigate the effects of an individual's appearance, and his decision with regard to the draft, on his evaluation by his peers and nonpeers. In this case, four fictitious students were created, and each was rated by two samples of students—one at a liberal college and one at a relatively conservative college—and by one sample of adults. If the reaction to the Hershey directive was indicative of the mood of the campuses, it might be expected that the draft resister, even though he broke the law, would be more highly evaluated than the nonresister. In addition, the use of the adult sample (the voters) would provide a means of determining whether the "cleaning for Gene" was an effective or superfluous tactic for political canvassers.

Method

SUBJECTS

The study was conducted between March and August of 1968. Four groups of subjects were used.

Columbia College Freshman Sample. First, 80 male freshmen at Columbia College were approached by a random door-to-door procedure in their dormitories and asked to cooperate in a brief psychological study that concerned the draft. The short time required to complete participation in the experiment and the provocative nature of the topic combined to achieve a high participation rate. Only 3 students out of 83 refused (2 of the 3 refusals were about to leave for a class, and the third was studying frantically for an imminent exam). No remuneration was offered to these or any other subjects.

Columbia College Senior Sample. This group consisted of 40 seniors at Columbia College. One-half of them were obtained by the same random door-to-door method in the dormitories, by which the freshman sample was recruited. The other half was obtained by telephoning seniors who lived in apartments and requesting that they come to the social psychology department at a scheduled hour.

Corning Community College Sample. This group consisted of 96 male and female students at Corning Community College in Corning, New York. These students tended to come from conservative, Catholic, working-class backgrounds as compared to the predominantly more affluent, Jewish families of Columbia

students. They were included in the study to allow a broader interpretation of
the opinions and stereotypes held by "college students."

The Adult Sample. For the purpose of comparing the obtained student responses with those of an older nonstudent population, several adult discussion
groups near Columbia University were asked to participate in the research
project. One, which was affiliated with a local Catholic church, agreed. This
sample consisted of 37 subjects, approximately half male and half female,
ranging in age from the mid-20s to the late 60s. None were college students at
the time of testing, though some had been to college.

PROCEDURE

Each subject was given a fictitious description of a college senior about to be
drafted; attached to each description was a photograph said to be a picture of
the senior described. All subjects read the following description of "Ralph" and
his problem:

> It is June 15, 1968. Ralph reflects over the past year, his senior year. It has been
> for him a year of much consideration about his future, a year of trying to come to a
> decision. The war in Vietnam has bothered Ralph considerably and—ever since
> General Hershey's directive in February eliminating graduate and occupational
> deferments—he has agonized over the alternatives open to him. Each of the alterna-
> tives is unappealing for different reasons: He does not want to fight in Vietnam
> because of his opposition to the war and his dissatisfaction with the general
> direction of America's foreign policy; he does not want to go to jail for 2 to 5 years
> because of the obvious unpleasantness of prison and the rejection, due to having
> been in prison, that could haunt him all his life; he does not want to emigrate to
> Canada because his family and friends are here in America, and he would like to
> remain an American citizen. But now it is mid-June and the decision has to be made.
> After long talks and extended thought, he realizes that there is only one alternative
> he can accept:

This paragraph then ended with one of the following four decisions by Ralph:

1. *Enlist:* "He will enlist in a branch of the service where he thinks chances of
   participating in actual combat would be minimal."
2. *Induct:* "He will, when inducted, go into the military and fight, if necessary, in Vietnam."
3. *Jail:* "He will refuse induction and, if convicted, serve his time in jail."
4. *Canada:* "He will leave as soon as possible for Canada."

To examine the effect of a stereotyped appearance, one of two different
passport pictures accompanied the description of Ralph. Both pictures were of
the same person. In one, the young man had a thick, bushy beard and fairly long
hair (Bearded Condition); in the other, he was clean shaven and had relatively

short hair (Clean-cut Condition). The pictures were taken in similar but not identical poses, but the most striking difference between the two was the presence or absence of a beard.

After reading the descriptive paragraph with one of the four endings, and looking at one of the two pictures, each subject was asked to rate the fictitious Ralph on 36 7-point bipolar adjective scales (e.g., sensitive—insensitive, authoritarian—democratic, brave—cowardly, good—bad, etc.). Twenty-three of the adjective scales were selected from a larger list developed by Pervin and Rubin (1967) in their work on the college dropout. The additional 13 scales were added by the present author because they seemed especially relevant to the question of the draft resister. After completing the ratings of Ralph, most subjects were asked to rate themselves on a scale of 1 to 7, dove to hawk, on their attitude toward the Vietnam War. This was done as a check to ensure a similar distribution of attitudes toward the war in all four decision X appearance conditions.

Definitions of the Term "Socially Desirable." In order to determine which of the 36 adjective pairs could be used to measure degree of liking, two additional samples were recruited—15 Columbia students and 78 additional Corning students. Each student was given the list of 36 semantic differential scales used in the study and asked to circle which pole, if either, he thought was "socially desirable." Any adjective circled by 80% or more of the subjects at each school was categorized as socially desirable for that respective sample. By this criterion, both Columbia and Corning students agreed on 14 of the 36 traits as socially desirable. In addition, each sample designated two other traits as socially desirable. These data are presented in Table A.1. In the analysis that follows only those 14 scales termed "socially desirable" by both college samples are considered.

Unfortunately, there was no opportunity to have a subsample of the church group rate the traits along the socially desirable dimension. For this reason, we utilized the 14 traits agreed upon by the Corning and Columbia samples as the dependent variable in the evaluation of Ralph throughout the study. While we cannot be sure that these were also the most appropriate items for the adult sample, the high degree of agreement between students from such diverse colleges gave us confidence in depending on them. The fact that previous researchers had found many of these same adjective scales to be rated as socially desirable further supported our use of them.

MODIFICATION OF PROCEDURE

The Columbia students participated in the study during March 1968, before the large demonstrations in the spring of that year, and, for them, Ralph was described as a senior at Columbia. However, because the Corning Community

Table A.1

Semantic Differential Scales of "Socially Desirable" Adjectives
Agreed upon by Columbia and Corning Students

authoritarian	1	2	3	4	5	6	7	democratic[a]
considerate[a]	1	2	3	4	5	6	7	inconsiderate
snobbish	1	2	3	4	5	6	7	friendly[a]
tolerant[a]	1	2	3	4	5	6	7	intolerant
good	1	2	3	4	5	6	7	bad
sensitive[a]	1	2	3	4	5	6	7	insensitive
concerned[a]	1	2	3	4	5	6	7	indifferent
creative[a]	1	2	3	4	5	6	7	uncreative
warm[a]	1	2	3	4	5	6	7	cold
open[a]	1	2	3	4	5	6	7	closed
honest[a]	1	2	3	4	5	6	7	dishonest
moral[a]	1	2	3	4	5	6	7	immoral
brave[a]	1	2	3	4	5	6	7	cowardly
brilliant[a]	1	2	3	4	5	6	7	stupid

[a]Socially desirable end.

College and the adult Catholic samples were tested in August and May respectively, after the Columbia disruptions, Ralph's identity was changed to that of a Yale student, to avoid the added political connotations that being designated a student at Columbia then entailed. In addition, because early data indicated few, if any, differences between the "Jail" and "Canada" conditions or between the "Enlist" and "Induct" conditions, the latter three samples (Columbia seniors, community college students, and adults) were tested using only the "Jail" and "Enlist" endings.

To summarize, four different samples of subjects read about and looked at a picture of a fictitious college senior. Two variables were manipulated, (1) what the senior decided to do about the draft and (2) what he looked like. Each subject rated this individual on 36 semantic differential scales, and then rated himself on his attitude toward the Vietnam War.

Results

COLUMBIA COLLEGE FRESHMEN AND SENIORS

A comparison of the responses of freshmen subjects with those of senior subjects indicates that although seniors considered themselves more "dovish" (t = 2.25, df = 118, $p < .05$) toward the Vietnam War, there were no major differences between freshmen and seniors on any of the independent variables. Accordingly, the responses of all Columbia students were pooled and analyzed together. The Jail-Canada conditions and the Enlist-Induct conditions were also grouped together to form, respectively, a "radical-acting" condition and a "conventional-acting" condition. A 2 X 2 analysis of variance (decision by appearance) was performed for each of the 14 socially desirable semantic differential scales.

When Ralph's decision was to resist, he was evaluated significantly more positively on 6 of the 14 scales than when his decision was to enlist in the army. Ralph the resister was rated, for example, more "brave," more "moral," more "brilliant," and more "sensitive" than Ralph the enlistee. In fact, this pattern was observed on 12 of 14 socially desirable traits. The means are presented in Table A.2. In order to determine if the resister was liked significantly more than the enlistee over all socially desirable adjectives, each individual's responses to the 14 scales were summed and these totals were used in a single 2 X 2 analysis of variance. As expected, the main effect of decision was significant at the .001 level ($F = 16.8, df = 1,116$).

The effect on Ralph's appearance was not as strong. Although on 12 of the 14 scales the Columbia subjects showed a preference for the bearded student, only two of the differences were significant—"creative" and "warm." These means are also shown in Table A.2. The overall analysis of variance, using total scores, produced a marginally significant main effect ($F = 2.94, df = 1,116, p < .10$), the preference being for the bearded Ralph.

CORNING COMMUNITY COLLEGE STUDENTS

Within the Corning sample the decision variable again produced a strong main effect. Whereas the Columbia students had been more laudatory toward the resister, the Corning students took the opposite point of view. The 2 X 2 analyses of variance reveal that they liked the enlistee significantly better than his radical counterpart on 4 of the 14 social desirability scales. They saw him as more "democratic," more "honest," more "moral," and more "good." The mean differences were in this same direction on 11 of the 14 scales (see Table A.3) and an analysis of variance of each individual's total score on the scales revealed a main effect of decision marginally significant at the .07 level ($F = 3.43, df = 1,92$).

The fictitious student's appearance produced no significant differences on any of the scales considered here. When the total scores on all scales were considered, the Corning subjects showed a slight tendency to prefer the bearded student, as did the subjects from Columbia College. The means are presented in Table A.3.

ADULT SAMPLE

The sample of Catholic adults shows a pattern very different from that of the two college samples. While analyses of the 14 scales reveal no significant main

Table A.2
Columbia Sample: Means on the Fourteen Desirability Scales

	Decision variable		Appearance variable	
	Resister (N=60) (bearded and cleancut combined)	Enlistee (N=60) (bearded and cleancut combined)	Bearded (N=60) (resister and enlistee combined)	Cleancut (N=60) (resister and enlistee combined)
Authoritarian-democratic	4.97[a]	4.73	4.82	4.88
Considerate-inconsiderate	5.23	4.80	4.02	4.02
Snobbish-friendly	4.68	4.68	4.77	4.60
Tolerant-intolerant	4.73	5.13	4.95	4.92
Good-bad	5.32	4.95	5.17	5.10
Sensitive-insensitive	5.88[b]	5.32	5.72	5.48
Concerned-indifferent	6.18[b]	5.57	5.95	5.80
Creative-uncreative	4.63[b]	3.72	4.50[b]	3.85
Warm-cold	4.63	4.32	4.73[b]	4.22
Open-closed	4.93	4.53	4.90	4.57
Honest-dishonest	5.62	5.23	5.50	5.38
Moral-immoral	5.88[b]	4.95	5.50	5.33
Brave-cowardly	5.30[b]	3.97	4.73	4.53
Brilliant-stupid	5.87[b]	5.52	4.75	4.63
Total scale score (item mean)	5.20[b]	4.70	5.07	4.88

[a]Mean score 7-point Likert Scale, social desirability end scored high. [b]
[b]Significant at $p < .05$ level.

Table A.3

Corning Sample: Means on the Fourteen Social Desirability Scales

	Decision variable		Appearance variable	
	Resister (N=48) (bearded and cleancut combined)	Enlistee (N=48) (bearded and cleancut combined)	Bearded (N=48) (resistor and enlistee combined)	Cleancut (N=48) (resistor and enlistee combined)
Authoritarian-democratic	4.25	4.94[a]	4.40	4.79
Considerate-inconsiderate	4.46	5.08	4.94	4.60
Snobbish-friendly	4.75	4.52	4.71	4.56
Tolerant-intolerant	3.51	4.12	3.87	3.79
Good-bad	4.54	5.04[a]	4.58	5.00
Sensitive-insensitive	5.71	5.83	5.75	5.79
Concerned-indifferent	5.83	6.15	6.06	5.92
Creative-uncreative	4.65	4.29	4.71	4.23
Warm-cold	4.42	4.52	4.50	4.44
Open-closed	4.92	5.02	4.87	5.06
Honest-dishonest	5.08	5.73[a]	5.25	5.56
Moral-immoral	5.04	5.62[a]	5.25	5.42
Brave-cowardly	3.83	4.21	4.23	5.81
Brilliant-stupid	5.08	5.06	4.98	5.17
Total scale score (item mean)	4.68	5.01	5.09	4.87

[a]Significant at $p<.05$ level.

161

effects for any of the traits, the *clean-cut* Ralph was seen as more socially desirable than the bearded Ralph on 12 of the 14 scales. Members of this sample showed no preference for either the resister or the enlistee, the differences being in one direction on 8 of the scales and in the other direction on the remaining 6. Thus, they did not, as did the two student samples, seem to base their evaluations on the nature of Ralph's behavior but on his outward appearance—at least to a stronger degree than did subjects from Columbia or Corning. However, an analysis of the adult sample using total scores on the 14 scales failed to produce a significant main effect for appearance, a major problem being the large within-cell variance, which was almost twice as large as that in the college samples.

THREE VARIABLE ANALYSIS

Since initial analyses within each sample pointed to different patterns of response to the fictitious Ralph, the data from all three samples were combined and a 2 X 2 X 3 analysis of variance (decision X appearance X sample) was performed on the total scores from the 14 scales. The interaction between draft decision and sample was significant ($F=6.25$, $df=2,241$, $p<.01$). As seen in Table A.4, the Columbia students liked the resister better, the Corning students liked the enlistee better, and the adults showed no preference for either.

INTERNAL ANALYSIS

While the interaction between the Columbia and Corning samples on the decision variable is intriguing, it can easily be explained in terms of differing attitudes toward the war on each of the campuses. In other words, assuming that Columbia students are relatively dovish and Corning students relatively hawkish, and assuming that those students who claim to be doves prefer the resister and those who claim to be hawks prefer the enlistee, the obtained results are predictable. However, as we shall see, while the first of these assumptions is correct, the second is not.

The difference between Columbia and Corning students in mean ratings on the 7-point dove-hawk scale was highly significant, the Columbia students, as expected, being more dovish.

An internal analysis, based on the subject's own attitude toward the war, was then performed. Those Columbia subjects who rated themselves 2 or 3 (dove) on the 7-point dove-hawk scale were compared with their schoolmates who had rated themselves 5 or 6 (hawk) on the scale, and Corning students who considered themselves dovish were compared with their hawkish schoolmates. Two separate 2 X 2 analyses of variance were performed—attitude and decision being

Table A.4
Social Desirability Scores as a Function of Draft Decision

	Decision to resist		Decision to enlist	
	$\bar{X}$	SD	$\bar{X}$	SD
Columbia College sample	5.20 (N=60)	.66	4.70 (N=60)	.56
Corning Community College sample	4.68 (N=48)	.84	5.01 (N=48)	.62
Adult sample	4.82 (N=19)	1.27	4.86 (N=18)	1.09

the independent variables. (Subjects with ratings of 1 or 7 on the scale were excluded because there was only one of the former in the Corning sample and none of the latter in the Columbia sample.)

If our initial assumption regarding the mediating role of attitudes is correct, we should expect to find a significant interaction effect on the decision and attitude variables for both samples. This is not the case. The cell means are shown in Table A.5. Although none of the effects are significant, the trends indicate

Table A.5
Social Desirability Ratings of Matched Groups of Doves and Hawks

	Dove		Hawk	
	$\bar{X}$	SD	$\bar{X}$	SD
Columbia				
Resister	5.18 (N=24)	.59	5.30 (N=4)	.28
Enlistee	4.79 (N=21)	.88	4.87 (N=5)	.23
Corning[a]				
Resister	5.19 (N=8)	.92	4.70 (N=7)	.77
Enlistee	5.20 (N=7)	.53	4.96 (N=8)	.64

[a]Only half of the Corning sample were asked to indicate their own attitude toward the war (dove-hawk), hence the small cell frequencies.

a clear preference by Columbia doves *and* hawks for the resister and a preference by Corning hawks *and* doves for the enlistee—the preference of doves being very slight. Thus the results of the study cannot wholly be attributable to the different distribution of Vietnam War attitudes at the two schools.

Yet it could be argued that a rating of 2 (the dove end of the scale) by someone at Corning is not equivalent to a rating of 2 by a Columbia student. It may actually represent a more hawkish position, since the ratings are probably relative to their peers, and the general sentiment at the community college was more hawkish. Therefore, the two subsamples are not comparable. There are two reasons for rejecting this argument. In the first place, one could just as easily postulate the existence of an assimilation-contrast phenomenon, in which case a rating of 2 at Corning could be very well represent a more dovish position than the same rating at Columbia. But the most damaging evidence against the attitudinal mediation notion is that the magnitude of preference for the resister on the part of both doves and hawks at Columbia is approximately equal, with the *hawks* having a small edge.

Discussion

The results of this study suggest that the political decision behind the "Clean for Gene" campaigning was well based. Although the members of the adult sample were not turned off by radical action, they responded negatively to Ralph when bearded compared to Ralph when shorn. If the patterns of the adults in our sample can be considered representative of adults voting in primaries in 1968, a clean-cut student is more highly evaluated.

The emphasis placed on appearance by the adults in our sample is sharply in contrast with the responses of the students at Corning and Columbia. Students at both schools expressed strong feelings about the hypothetical student's behavior but were relatively unconcerned with his appearance. The concern with beards probably does not represent a general conservatism in the adult sample, as these same adults evaluated the radical-acting student more positively than did the Corning students. Also, they belonged to a church group located near Columbia University, a strongly Democratic-voting district and, therefore, were probably representative of a middle-aged liberal viewpoint. The fact that the adults relied on appearance to make judgments while the students based their judgments on action seems to indicate a qualitative difference between adults and students and not differing degrees on a continuum of sophistication-radicalism. In this difference of priorities lies a true generation gap.

By rejecting appearance as a criterion on which to judge a person, the students seem to be reaffirming their dislike of superficialities in personal relations. The outcry against the hypocrisy of the older generation receives support from these findings. Probably most adults when directly questioned would deny that a person's appearance is given more weight than his actions in making judgments about him; yet looks were the important cue in this situation for our sample of adults. The immediate challenge of Ralph's long hair and beard may have been more threatening to their own value systems than the relative remoteness of the revolution that Ralph as a resister potentially represented.

Like the adults, the respondents from the college samples reacted to the characteristic of Ralph most relevant to themselves, that is, his behavior vis-à-vis the draft; but the nature of the life style on each campus seems to have dictated the direction of their responses to this variable. Many students at Columbia go on to some type of graduate school after completing college. For these students, Hershey's directive in February 1968 canceling graduate school deferments could have portended a change in career or, more importantly, a change in their approach to the institution of government. For the first time, especially for this relatively affluent population, the government's actions would directly and deeply affect their lives. The admired response to this threat on the Columbia campus appeared to be the anti-Establishment one of resisting. While Hershey's directive did not in one thrust radicalize the Columbia campus, it did make the Vietnam War, already the biggest political issue at the school, more tangible and more heinous to college students. By endorsing Ralph when he behaved in an anti-Establishment manner, students were showing their support for radical tactics over traditional ones.

The situation was undoubtedly different on the Corning campus. Few students there aspire to graduate school, so for them the draft had always been a very real issue. If they had not already served, most of the male respondents in the sample probably included the armed forces as an inevitable part of their future, and the women probably all had friends or family who had been or were expecting to be in the army. The Corning students' preference for the enlistee over the resister appears to represent an affirmation of themselves and their life style. Beards and long hair as symbols of the youth culture seem to be more widely and quickly assimilable than breaking the law.

These differences in outlook between the students at the two colleges reflect and are reflected by the differing ambience at those colleges. Columbia, with its academic tradition, fosters a community spirit that is enhanced by the high percentage of students living on or near the campus and by having students who can devote their full time to the university. Not surprisingly, there was greater homogeneity of responses at Columbia; students who rated themselves as doves as well as those who rated themselves as hawks shared a preference for the resister. At Corning, where students commute from wide distances and school is often an extracurricular activity rather than the core one, attitudes are probably more independent of the institutional context. As a result, the dovish respondents there had a somewhat weaker preference for Ralph the enlistee than their hawkish school-mates.

The academic training a student receives at Columbia encourages him to analyze problems in cosmic terms. Consequently, he may tend to see the question of the draft as an ideological one, and because of his relative affluence, he can then respond to it without concern for possible future of repercussions. From such a "politically relevant" ivory tower, disapproval of the Vietnam War leads inevitably to resistance. The Corning student, however, cannot afford to be idealistic. In most cases he attends college to obtain skills that will permit him upward societal mobility. Fleeing to Canada or having a prison record would present such formidable obstacles to the attainment of his career goals (already hampered by his relatively poor background) that these alternatives are inconceivable even at the abstract level accorded by the experiment. His personal problems require pragmatic solutions; he cannot afford the potentially dangerous repercussions of draft resistance.

Appendix B-1
Item Means and Part-Whole Correlations for the Original Items of the New Left Scale[1]

r_{iRS}[2]	Scale[3]	Mean[4]		
.750	R+	3.18	86.	The "Establishment" unfairly controls every aspect of our lives; we can never be free until we are rid of it.
.685	R+	3.26	62.	You can never achieve freedom within the framework of contemporary American society.
.658	R+	4.16	18.	The United States need a complete restructuring of its basic institutions.
.650	R+	3.09	20.	A mass revolutionary party should be created.

continued

[1] The 20 New Left (R) items with the highest part-whole correlations constituted the shortened measure of New Left ideology used in the friendship study discussed in Chapter 7 and in subsequent chapters.

[2] r_{iRS} is the cross-product moment correlation of each subject's score on each item (i) with his total score on the 62-items of New Left ideology. N=153 Columbia College freshmen.

[3] The following code has been used to indicate the scale from which the item was originally taken.

R = New Left   DT = Distrust of people
AN = Affirmative-Negative   TM = Traditional Moralism
DP = Duplicity (Machiavellian Tactics)

The last four scales were taken from the FacMac Scale (Christie & Lehmann, 1970).
The signs following each letter indicate the direction of scoring:
+ = an agree response scored high   − = a disagree response scored high

[4] Mean signifies the mean response for the sample on that item. The response varied from 1 ("disagree strongly") to 7 ("agree strongly"). 4 was labeled "no opinion."

$r_{iRS}{}^2$ Scale[3] Mean[4]

.622	R+	4.95	32.	Authorities must be put in an intolerable position so they will be forced to respond with repression and thus show their illegitimacy.
.582	R+	3.82	36.	The solutions for comtemporary problems lie in striking at their roots, no matter how much destruction might occur.
.549	R+	4.16	17.	Disruption is preferable to dialogue for changing our society.
.549	R+	4.16	16.	Even though institutions have worked well in the past, they must be destroyed if they are not effective now.
.524	R+	4.05	14.	The structure of our society is such that self-alienation is inevitable.
.510	R+	6.05	31.	Sexual behavior should be bound by mutual feelings, not by formal and legal ties.
.509	R+	5.16	88.	A problem with most older people is that they have learned to accept society as it is, not as it should be.
.498	R+	3.67	4.	The bureaucracy of American society makes it impossible to live and work spontaneously.
−.493	R−	4.93	29.	Radicals of the left are as much a threat to the rights of the individual as are the radicals of the right.
.474	R+	3.77	50.	While man has great potential for good, society brings out primarily the worst in him.
.467	R+	1.68	66.	The processes of rebuilding society are of less immediate importance than the processes of destroying it.
.463	R+	3.68	61.	The political structure of the Soviet Union is more like that of the United States than that of Red China.
.462	R+	2.90	24.	The streets are a more appropriate medium for change in our society than printing presses.
−.460	R−	4.75	28.	Competition encourages excellence.

continued

r_{iRS}[2] Scale[3] Mean[4]

.460	R+	3.07	78.	Marriage unfairly restricts one's personal freedom.
-.459	R-	3.88	88.	The right to private property is sacred.
.450	AN+	3.78	1.	Most people in government are not really interested in the problems of the average man.
.448	R+	2.74	72.	No one should be punished for violating a law which he feels is immoral.
.447	TM-	5.43	35.	If it weren't for the rebellious ideas of youth there would be less progress in the world.
-.438	R-	4.74	89.	The courts are a useful vehicle for responsible change.
-.434	R-	5.82	83.	There are legitimate channels for reform which must be exhausted before attempting disruption.
.428	R+	2.93	37.	You learn more from 10 minutes in a political protest than 10 hours of research in a library.
-.423	R-	4.63	22.	Although our society has to be changed, violence is not a justified means.
-.420	R-	5.66	51.	Society needs some legally based authority in order to prevent chaos.
-.417	R-	4.56	43.	Representative democracy can respond effectively to the needs of the people.
-.413	R-	2.46	7.	Police should not hesitate to use force to maintain order.
.410	R+	4.69	34.	Real participatory democracy should be the basis for a new society.
-.404	R-	2.49	13.	If people worked hard at their jobs, they would reap the full benefits of our society.
.404	R+	4.29	54.	Groups with a formal structure tend to stifle creativity among their members.
.397	R+	4.07	47.	A social scientist should not separate his political responsibilities from his professional role.
.397	R+	3.33	38.	People should not do research which can be used in ways which are contrary to the social good.

continued

$r_{iRS}{}^2$ Scale[3] Mean[4]

−.396	R−	4.27	65.	Abrupt reforms in society usually lead to such a severe backlash that they will be self-defeating.
.395	TM−	5.98	40.	People ought to pay more attention to new ideas, even if they seem to go against the American way of life.
−.387	R−	4.71	74.	Traditions serve a useful social function by providing stability and continuity.
−.367	R−	2.43	46.	The very existence of our long-standing social norms demonstrates their value.
.366	R+	3.58	53.	If the structure of our society becomes nonrepressive, people will be happy.
.360	R+	2.77	75.	The distinction between public and private life is unnecessary.
.358	AN+	3.87	12.	Most people don't realize how much our lives are controlled by plots hatched in secret places.
−.346	R−	5.14	57.	Compromise is essential for progress.
.337	R+	2.61	44.	Extensive reform in society only serves to perpetuate the evils; it will never solve problems.
−.331	R−	3.52	3.	Voting must be a pragmatic rather than moral decision.
−.328	R−	5.29	27.	Anyone who violates the law for reasons of conscience should be willing to accept the legal consequences.
−.308	R−	4.65	70.	It is possible to modify our institutions so that the blacks can be incorporated on an equal basis into our contemporary society.
−.299	DT−	4.36	49.	If you try hard enough, you can usually get what you want.
.297	R+	3.41	25.	Although men are intrinsically good, they have developed institutions which force them to act in opposition to their basic nature.
.279	R+	2.41	58.	Educational institutions should espouse political doctrines.
.279	AN+	2.90	77.	The biggest difference between most criminals and

continued

r_{iRS}[2] Scale[3] Mean[4]

			other people is that criminals are stupid enough to get caught.
−.271	TM+	2.09	60. Every person should have complete faith in a supernatural power whose decisions he obeys without question.
.259	TM−	5.01	19. The findings of science may some day show that many of our most cherished beliefs are wrong.
.259	TM−	5.30	73. People suffering from incurable diseases should have the choice of being put painlessly to death.
−.259	R−	4.21	81. Change in our society should be based primarily on popular elections.
−.250	R−	3.69	6. A minority must never be allowed to impose its will on a majority.
−.244	R−	4.42	82. Spontaneity is often an excuse for irresponsibility.
.238	R+	4.43	63. An individual can find his true identity only by detaching himself from formal ideologies.
.236	DP−	4.80	55. When you ask someone to do something for you, it is best to give the real reasons for wanting it rather than giving reasons which carry more weight.
.235	TM−	4.95	5. Books and movies ought to give a more realistic picture of life even if they show that evil sometimes triumphs over good.
−.235	R−	3.59	85. Being put in positions of leadership brings out the best in men.
−.235	DT−	3.96	21. Most people can still be depended on to come through in a pinch.
.230	R+	2.87	52. Political factions cannot cooperate with each other without sacrificing their integrity.
.225	R+	3.88	79. It is more important that people be involved in the present rather than concerned with the past or the future.
−.224	DT−	2.17	41. Most people who get ahead in the world lead clean, moral lives.
.221	DT+	3.45	9. No sane, normal, decent person could even think of hurting a close friend or relative.

continued

$r_{iRS}{}^2$ Scale[3] Mean[4]

.218	R+	4.06	48.	A commitment to action is more socially relevant than a commitment to any specific philosophy.
−.213	R−	5.67	30.	Commitment to a meaningful career is a very important part of a man's life.
−.197	R−	3.07	26.	One's personal life can be kept separate from one's political life.
−.196	DP+	3.02	64.	It is wise to flatter important people.
−.177	R−	4.94	2.	A group without a clear-cut pattern of leadership cannot function effectively.
.171	DP−	5.60	15.	All in all, it is better to be humble and honest than to be important and dishonest.
−.153	DP+	1.67	39.	Next to health, money is the most important thing in life.
.147	R+	1.88	10.	Freedom of expression should be denied to racist and neofascistic movements.
.120	R−	5.71	23.	Provocation of the police should only be a by-product, not a goal, of mass action.
−.115	R−	3.94	69.	A liberal society is more conducive to revolutionary change than is a fascistic one.
−.108	R−	5.40	59.	We must strive for the democratization of decision-making bodies within the existing government.
−.101	DT−	3.04	76.	Most people will go out of their way to help someone else.
−.088	AN+	3.95	56.	Anyone who completely trusts anyone else is asking for trouble.
.088	R+	2.05	11.	The only way to combat violence is to use violent means.
.064	DP−	4.00	71.	Honesty is the best policy in all cases.
.052	DT−	3.14	87.	Most men are brave.
.052	DT−	3.84	80.	Most people are basically good and kind.
.043	R+	3.88	67.	You should always be candid with your friends even though you may hurt their feelings.
.042	TM−	5.24	84.	Most honest people admit to themselves that they have sometimes hated their parents.

continued

r_{iRS}[2] Scale[3] Mean[4]

−.030	AN+	2.55	33.	Most of our social problems could be solved if we could somehow get rid of the immoral, crooked, and feeble-minded people.
−.029	DP+	3.58	45.	The best way to handle people is to tell them what they want to hear.
−.024	DP−	3.01	8.	There is no excuse for lying to someone else.
−.016	AN+	3.56	42.	Generally speaking, men won't work hard unless they're forced to do so.
−.015	AN+	3.89	90.	It is safest to assume that all people have a vicious streak and it will come out when they are given a chance.

Appendix B-2a
Revised Version of the New Left Scale[1]

Instructions

Circle only one alternative for each item on your answer sheet. Listed below are a number of statements. We have collected them from a variety of sources and there are no right or wrong answers. You will probably disagree with some items and agree with others. We are interested in the extent to which you agree or disagree with such matters of opinion.

Read each statement carefully. Then indicate the extent to which you agree or disagree by circling the corresponding alternative on your answer sheet. The number of the alternatives and their meanings are:

If you disagree strongly	circle 1
If you disagree somewhat	circle 2
If you disagree slightly	circle 3
If you have no opinion	circle 4
If you agree slightly	circle 5
If you agree somewhat	circle 6
If you agree strongly	circle 7

First impressions are usually best in such matters. Read each statement, decide if you agree or disagree and the strength of your opinion, and then circle the

[1] Items marked with an asterisk are those used in the version of the New Left scale given to the high school students. Most items are from the New Left Philosophy, Revolutionary Tactics, and Traditional Moralism factor scales. Numbers in parenthesis represent the item number on the original scale.

appropriate alternative on the answer sheet. Read the items carefully, but work as rapidly as you can. *Give your opinion on every statement.*

If you find that the numbers to be used in answering do not adequately indicate you own opinion, use the one that is *closest* to the way you feel.

*1. If all people were free to do whatever they wanted, everyone would be happy. (53)

*2. If people worked hard at their jobs, they would get the full benefits of our society. (13)

*3. Groups that are highly organized prevent their members from being creative. (54)

4. Most people in government are not really interested in the problems of the average man. (1)

*5. You learn more from 10 minutes in a political protest than from 10 hours of research in a library. (37)

6. Most of our social problems could be solved if we could somehow get rid of the immoral, crooked, and feeble-minded people. (33)

7. It is dangerous to allow people with extreme views complete freedom of speech. (10)

*8. Scientists should only do research which will be used for man's benefit. (38)

9. The best way to solve social problems is through the courts. (89)

*10. The society man has created makes him act against his basic tendency to be good. (50)

*11. No one is free to do what he wants in America today. (62)

12. The strict organization of American society makes it impossible to live and work without constantly planning ahead. (4)

13. It is wise to flatter important people. (64)

14. All in all, it is better to be humble and honest than to be important and dishonest. (15)

*15. Even though institutions, like the schools, the courts, the church and the government have worked in the past, they must be destroyed if they no longer work well. (16)

*16. Before strikes and demonstrations are used to bring about change, we should try to change America by laws. (83)

17. Most people will go out of their way to help someone else. (76)

18. When you ask someone to do something for you, it is best to give the real

reasons for wanting it rather than giving reasons that carry more weight. (55)

*19. A mass revolutionary party should be created. (20)

20. It is better to support a man who can get things done rather than one who is completely honest. (3)

21. The findings of science may some day show that many of our most cherished beliefs are wrong. (19)

*22. Police should not hesitate to use force to keep order. (7)

*23. There always has to be a little give and take if you want to improve things. (57)

*24. Changes in our society should be based primarily on popular elections. (81)

25. Most men are brave. (87)

*26. People who want to change society completely are as dangerous as those who don't want to change it at all. (29)

27. It is more important that people live in the present rather than worry about the past or the future. (79)

*28. If someone breaks a law because he thinks it is wrong, he should be willing to stand trial. (27)

*29. Real participatory democracy should be the basis for a new society. (34)

*30. Important leaders must be put on the spot so that it is clear to everyone that they don't understand the real problems. (32)

31. No sane, normal, decent person could even think of hurting a close friend or relative. (9)

32. We must strive for the democratization of decision-making bodies within the existing government. (59)

*33. If social customs have lasted for a long time, we know they must be good. (46)

*34. Scientists and teachers should never do work which is not true to their personal political beliefs. (47)

35. Being put in positions of leadership brings out the best in men. (85)

*36. Competition encourages excellence. (28)

37. Most people can still be depended on to come through in a pinch. (21)

*38. By making changes in our government, schools and courts, blacks can have the same rights and opportunities as whites. (70)

*39. Our institutions are organized in such a way that any thoughtful person feels uncomfortable when he thinks about society. (14)

40. It is safest to assume that all people have a vicious streak and it will come out when they are given a chance. (90)

*41. American institutions like the government, the church, the courts, and the schools needs to be changed completely. (18)

42. Anyone who completely trusts anyone else is asking for trouble. (56)

43. Most people who get ahead in the world lead clean, moral lives. (41)

44. Most people don't realize how much our lives are controlled by plots hatched in secret places. (12)

45. The best way to handle people is to tell them what they want to hear. (45)

46. As long as no one is hurt, our sex lives should be guided by our feelings rather than be guided by rules and laws. (31)

*47. A problem with older people is that they have learned to accept America as it is, instead of as it should be. (88)

*48. Although American society needs to be changed, violence is not a good way to change it. (22)

49. Next to health, money is the most important thing in life. (39)

*50. Demonstrations are better than discussions for getting things changed in America. (17)

*51. The "Establishment" unfairly controls every aspect of our lives; we can never be free until we are rid of it. (86)

52. Every person should have complete faith in a supernatural power whose decisions he obeys without question. (60)

53. People ought to pay more attention to new ideas, even if they seem to go against the American way of life. (40)

54. Most people are basically good and kind. (80)

55. In a democracy where there are elected representatives, all the needs of the people can be satisfied. (43)

*56. Lots of changes in American society will only continue the present wrongs, they will never solve problems. (44)

57. If you try hard enough, you can usually get what you want. (49)

*58. The right to have personal property is sacred. (68)

*59. Although most men are basically good, they are usually put in situations where they have to do things they don't really believe in. (25)

60. If it weren't for the rebellious ideas of youth, there would be less progress in the world. (35)

Appendix B-2b
Comparison of Original and Revised Versions of the New Left Scale

Approximately one-half of the students in each of the classes at Suffolk and Corning Community Colleges were given the revised version of the 60-item New Left scale. The other half were given the original version. A comparison of scale scores between the two versions was made. t tests between the scores on the original and revised versions for each school were performed. Only one of the 10 comparisons was significant. At Corning Community College, students who took the revised form of the scale scored higher on Revolutionary Tactics than students who took the original version ($t = 2.20$, $df = 65$, $p < .05$). Although this evidence is not sufficient to conclude that the two versions are substantially different, inspection of the means on the other factors suggests a difference. For 7 of the 10 comparisons, scores of respondents given the revised version were more radical than those given the original version. In sum, the data lead us to believe that identical scores on the two versions are not indicative of identical levels of radicalism.

	N	Traditional Moralism		Machiavellian Tactics		Machiavellian Cynicism		New Left Philosophy		Revolutionary Tactics	
		$\bar{X}$	SD	$\bar{X}$	SD	$\bar{X}$	SD	$\bar{X}$	SD	$\bar{X}$	SD
Suffolk–original	32	3.37	.85	3.65	.70	3.97	.93	3.90	.78	2.80	.74
Suffolk–revised	35	3.24	.60	3.69	.82	4.32	.86	3.71	.76	2.88	.56
Corning–original	34	3.22	.89	3.46	.58	3.71	.66	3.92	.77	2.79	.78
Corning–revised	33	3.10	.83	3.27	.72	3.97	.76	3.87	.73	3.19	.68

Appendix B-3

Fifteen-Item New Left Scale Used in Yankelovich-CBS National College Sample Survey

The following items (all from the original version of New Left scale) were used:

1. Competition encourages excellence.
2. The right to private property is sacred.
3. Society needs some legally based authority in order to prevent chaos.
4. Compromise is essential for progress.
5. The "Establishment" unfairly controls every aspect of our lives; we can never be free until we are rid of it.
6. A mass revolutionary party should be created.
7. Authorities must be put in an intolerable position so they will be forced to respond with repression and thus show their illegitimacy.
8. Disruption is preferable to discussing issues for changing our society.
9. Sexual behavior should be bound by mutual feelings, not by formal and legal ties.
10. A minority should never be allowed to impose its will on the majority.
11. There are legitimate channels for reform which must be exhausted before attempting disruption.
12. Today, rebuilding society is of less immediate importance than destroying it.

13. Radicals of the left are as much a threat to the rights of the individual as are radicals of the right.

14. The American system of representative democracy can respond effectively to the needs of the people.

15. Man is basically good, but our society brings out the worst in him.

SCORING

Items 1-4. Respondents indicated solely whether they agreed or disagreed (2-point scale). In order to make the item means comparable with those for the samples given a 7-point scale, responses in the radical direction were weighted "6" ("somewhat agree") and those in the conservative direction were weighted "2" ("somewhat disagree").

Items 5-15. Respondents were given a 3-point scale: "strongly agree," "partially agree," "strongly disagree." Weightings were as follows: In the radical direction, "strongly agree" weighted "7," "partially agree" weighted "5," and "strongly disagree" weighted "2."

Appendix C-1

Background Questionnaire Given to Columbia College Panel Sample When Freshmen (Fall 1968)

1. Date of birth _____

2. Intended major _____

3. Intended career _____

4. Are you 1. white 2. black
   3. other _____

5. Where will you be living this semester? (Circle)
   1. Dormitory (which one?) _____   2. With parents

6. What did you do last summer? (If job, please describe.)

7. The following have been suggested as possible goals of a university. Which do you think should be given greatest priority? (Please rank all choices, giving *1* for the one you think is most important and *5* for the one which is least important. If you feel that one or more of these statements should not be a goal of a university, give it a rank of *0*.)

   _____ To provide a place for learning which is free from the pressures and of the larger society

   _____ To provide training directly applicable to the careers of its students

   _____ To provide a forum for the critical analysis of all aspects of the larger society

   _____ To act as a base of social action through implementation and and experimentation with new solutions to social problems

   _____ To act as a base for political action in the larger society

8. Under most circumstances in a political crisis on a university campus, which tactics do you think students should use? (Please rank the following in order of preference, giving *1* for the best tactic and *5* for the least preferred tactic.

181

If you feel one or more of the tactics should never be used, give it a rank of
0.)

_____ Allow the administration to resolve the problems

_____ Negotiations through official student groups

_____ Elections and referendums on the issues involved

_____ Peaceful protest through petitions and rallies

_____ Direct and forceful confrontation of the opposition

9. Under most circumstances in the larger society, which of the following
tactics do you favor? (Rank as above.)

_____ Allow the government to resolve problems

_____ Referendums and plebiscites on specific issues

_____ Peaceful protest through petitions and rallies

_____ Direct and forceful confrontation of the opposition

10. How much decision-making power should the following groups have in
making major University policies such as expansion, discipline, and curri-
culum? (Rank according to how much power: 1st, 2nd, etc. Two groups
given same rank indicates equal power. 0 = no power.)

_____ Students   _____ Faculty   _____ Undecided

_____ Administration   _____ Trustees

11. In matters affecting the community around Columbia, such as plans for the
use of land, relocation of tenants, etc., how much decision-making power
should the following groups have? (Rank as above.)

_____ Local residents   _____ The city

_____ The university   _____ Undecided

12. Please match the following names with their appropriate definition by
putting the correct number of the definition in the blank next to the name.
There is only one definition which is correct for each name. All names can
be matched with the definitions.

_____ SAS

_____ Cox Commission

_____ Rudd

_____ SRU

_____ Hamilton

_____ Vilardi

_____ Ad Hoc Committee

_____ Students for Columbia
University

1. Organization of students and alumni
2. Chairman of Students for Democratic Society
3. Committee to stop SDS activities
4. Chairman of Students for a Free
Campus
5. Faculty committee negotiating between students and administration
6. Building occupied by black students
7. Outside committee studying the
events of the spring demonstrations

8. Committee established by Kirk to discipline strikers
9. Committee of students studying proposals for changes in University structure
10. Chairman of the Independent Faculty Committee
11. Organization of black students
12. Chairman of Majority Coalition

13. During the crisis at Columbia last spring several issues were raised. Please indicate your feelings toward them by circling the appropriate number for each issue.

	Support	Neutral	Oppose	Don't have enough information to say
a. Amnesty for demonstrators	1	2	3	4
b. Stopping construction of gym	1	2	3	4
c. Dropping legal charges against demonstrators arrested at gym site	1	2	3	4
d. Disaffiliation from Institute for Defense Analysis (IDA)	1	2	3	4
e. Elimination of rule against indoor demonstrations	1	2	3	4
f. Student discipline judged by bipartite committee of students and faculty	1	2	3	4
g. Fundamental restructuring of Columbia	1	2	3	4
h. Tactics of the demonstrators	1	2	3	4

14. Which of the following sources of information have been most influential in formulating your opinions about the Columbia crisis last spring? Please rank.

_____ *Columbia Spectator* (student newspaper)
_____ *New York Times*
_____ Local newspapers
_____ Radical newspapers
_____ Magazines (list)_____
_____ Magazines (list)_____

_____ WKCR radio (student radio station)
_____ Other radio and TV stations
_____ Columbia students
_____ Parents and other friends
_____ Own observations
_____ Meetings

15. Do you believe that democratic channels can be utilized effectively for the expression of dissent in this society? In Columbia University?

	Most of the time	Some of the time	Never	Don't know
The society	1	2	3	4
The university	1	2	3	4

Please indicate whether you agree or disagree with the following statements.

16. In general the American government has been responsive to the needs and desires of its citizens.

    1   2   3   4   5
strongly   mildly   mildly   strongly   don't
agree   agree   disagree   disagree   know

17. Law and order must be established before the United States can start to solve its internal problems.

    1   2   3   4   5
strongly   mildly   mildly   strongly   don't
agree   agree   disagree   disagree   know

18. Movements like the National Liberation Front should be supported.

    1   2   3   4   5
strongly   mildly   mildly   strongly   don't
agree   agree   disagree   disagree   know

19. The exploitation of certain groups is an *inherent* part of our present society.

    1   2   3   4   5
strongly   mildly   mildly   strongly   don't
agree   agree   disagree   disagree   know

20. Disruptive acts are justified if they interfere with the war effort in Vietnam.

    1   2   3   4   5
strongly   mildly   mildly   strongly   don't
agree   agree   disagree   disagree   know

21. If *10* represents the most radical student, *0* represents a slightly liberal student, -10 the most conservative student, where would you place yourself?

-10 -9 -8 -7 -6 -5 -4 -3 -2 -1 0 1 2 3 4 5 6 7 8 9 10
Conservative   *Liberal*   *Radical*

22. Which of the announced candidates for the presidency do you now or have you ever favored? (Circle all that apply.)

1. Cleaver	6. McCarthy	11. Rockefeller
2. Gregory	7. McGovern	12. Wallace
3. Halstead	8. Charlene Mitchell	13. Undecided
4. Humphrey	9. Nixon	14. Other _____
5. R. F. Kennedy	10. Reagan	15. None

23. Have you worked for the candidate of your choice?

          1. No   2. Yes   If yes, how many hours? _____

24. Have you contributed money to the candidate of your choice?

          1. No   2. Yes

25. Have you participated in any of the following activities of the Civil Rights movement? (Circle all that apply.)

0 None	4 Tutoring (how often weekly?)_____
1 Signed petitions	5 Voter registration (for how long?)_____
2 Contributed money	6 Demonstrations and marches (which ones?)
3 Arrested	_____
	_____
	7 Other_____

26. Have you participated in any of the following activities in the peace movement?

0 None	6 Worked at draft counselling center
1 Signed petitions	(How much?)_____
2 Contributed money	7 Teach-ins (how many?)_____
3 Vietnam summer	8 Other_____
4 Arrested	

5 Demonstrations and marches (circle those attended)
    a. April 15, 1967, N.Y.C.
    b. October 1967, Pentagon
    c. April 27, 1968, N.Y.C.
    d. Induction centers
    e. Other (specify date and place)

27. Which of the following groups did you belong to in high school? (Circle the numbers which apply and write in degree of involvement. 3=very involved, 1=not involved)

                              Involvement   Offices held

    1. Fraternity
    2. Student publication
    3. Service organization
    4. Athletics
    5. Political action group (name)
    6. Student government (list committees)

28. Do you intend to join any of these groups at Columbia?

          1. No   2. Yes   If yes, which ones? _____

29. In high school did you participate in any student groups which were interested in changing the organization or rules pertaining to:

	Yes	No	No group in my school	Offices held[a]
1. Curriculum	1	2	3	
2. Student government	1	2	3	
3. Student conduct (e.g., hair length)	1	2	3	
4. Discipline of students	1	2	3	
5. Student newspaper	1	2	3	
6. Other _____	1	2	3	

[a]If yes, please describe your activities briefly.

30. While you were in high school, did you participate in any political activity which could have led to any of the consequences listed?

	No	Yes
1. Probation	1	2
2. Suspension	1	2
3. Explusion	1	2
4. Other discipline	1	2

31. While at Columbia do you think you would be willing to participate in any political activities which might involve:

	Yes	No	Maybe	Don't know
1. Probation at school	1	2	3	4
2. Suspension from school	1	2	3	4
3. Explusion from school	1	2	3	4
4. Arrest	1	2	3	4

32. If you were about to be drafted, would you:
    1 Go into the service   3 Refuse induction and risk jail
    2 Try to appeal through legal channels   4 Leave the country

33. Was Columbia your first choice?   1. Yes   2 No
    If no, where would you have preferred to go? _____

34. In general, how satisfied are you about going to Columbia?

1	2	3	4
extremely satisfied	somewhat satisfied	somewhat dissatisfied	extremely dissatisfied

35. Please describe briefly and candidly your reasons for applying to Columbia.

36. While at Columbia, how do you plan to use your time? Please rank all choices starting with *1* for the activity to which you expect to devote the most time. Give *0* to those activities to which you expect to devote no time.

_____ Job   _____ Hobbies (e.g.,   _____ Campus political

_____ Studying   art, music)   activities

_____ Fraternity   _____ Athletics   _____ Outside political

_____ Other   _____ Religious activities   activities

(please specify) _____   _____ Social life (e.g.,

                                                dating, parties)

Appendix C-2
Background Questionnaire Given to Columbia College Panel Sample When Sophomores (Fall 1969)

1. Date of birth _____   2. Intended major _____

3. Intended career _____

4. Where did you live the majority of time during the 5 years before coming to college?

   _____   _____
   (town)   (state)

5. What type of high school did you attend? (Circle the appropriate number.)
   1 Public school   2 Private day school   3 Private boarding school
   4 Parochial school

6. Thinking back to your *economic* circumstances when you were a child, would you say you felt:
   1 very secure   2 fairly secure   3 not very secure

7. What about now? Would you say that *you* feel financially:
   1 very secure   2 fairly secure   3 not very secure

8. Do your parents give you moral support in your political position even though you may disagree with you?

	Yes	No
Mother	1	2
Father	1	2

9. Does your parents' political position tend to alter in any way your political commitment?

1 decrease it   2 increase it   3 no effect

10. Do your parents now or have they ever engaged in political activities?

	Yes	No
Mother	1	2
Father	1	2

If yes, please describe the general type of activity?

Activity	Approximate date
_____	_____
_____	_____

11. Circle the highest education level reached by each of your parents.

	Mother	Father
0–6 years	1	1
7–9 years	2	2
10–11 years	3	3
12 years (high school graduate)	4	4
13–15 years (some college)	5	5
16 years (college graduate)	6	6
17 years or more (graduate work)	7	7

12. The following have been suggested as possible goals of a university. Which do you think should be given greatest priority? (Please rank all choices, giving *1* for the one you think is most important and *5* for the one which is least important. If you feel that one or more of these statements should not be a goal of a university, give it a rank of *0*.)

_____ To provide a place for learning which is free from the pressures and influences of the larger society

_____ To provide training directly applicable to careers of its students

_____ To provide a forum for the critical analysis of all aspects of the larger society

_____ To act as a base of social action through implementation and experimentation with new solutions to social problems

_____ To act as a base for political action in the larger society

13. Under most circumstances in a political crisis on a university campus, which tactics do you think students should use? (Please rank the following in order of preference, giving *1* for the best tactic and *5* for the least preferred tactic.

If you feel one or more of the tactics should never be used, give it a rank of *0*.)

_____ Allow the administration to resolve the problems

_____ Negotiations through official student groups

_____ Elections and referendums on the issues involved

_____ Peaceful protest through petitions and rallies

_____ Direct and forceful confrontation of the opposition

14. Under most circumstances in the larger society, which of the following tactics do you favor? (Rank as above.)

_____ Allow the government to resolve problems

_____ Referendums and plebiscites on specific issues

_____ Peaceful protest through petitions and rallies

_____ Direct and forceful confrontation of the opposition

15. Which of the following political involvements interest you the most?

    1 issues   2 tactics   3 education others   4 no interest in politics

16. In what ways has this interest changed since last year?

    I am more interested in: 1 tactics   2 issues   3 educating others
    I am less interested in: 1 tactics   2 issues   3 educating others

17. What political issues interest you the most?

    Has this changed since you have been at Columbia?   1 No   2 Yes
    If yes, how?

18. How confident are you that your political activities (or lack of them) are justified?

    1 extremely   2 fairly   3 ambivalent   4 not very   5 not confident
       confident   confident   confident   at all

19. Circle the number which most closely reflects your involvement in the following events:

	Partici- pated in opposi- tion to	Disap- proved of	Neutral observer	Sympa- thized with	Partici- pated in	Indif- ferent
a. Registration demonstra- tions, Sept. 1968	1	2	3	4	5	6
b. Suit against Columbia Trustees concerning						

	Partici-pated in opposi-tion to	Disap-proved of	Neutral observer	Sympa-thized with	Partici-pated in	Indif-ferent
demonstrations of spring 1968	1	2	3	4	5	6
c. NROTC teach-in (Dodge, Hamilton) Feb. 1969	1	2	3	4	5	6
d. NROTC counterrally	1	2	3	4	5	6
e. Community demon-strations and marches to stop Columbia expansion	1	2	3	4	5	6
f. One-day SDS strike (March 28, 1969)	1	2	3	4	5	6
g. Rally to support black sit-in demanding Interim Board	1	2	3	4	5	6
h. Expansion Committee sit-in, in Hamilton, April 1969	1	2	3	4	5	6
i. Philosophy Hall sit-in	1	2	3	4	5	6
j. Operation Evacuation, April 22, 1969	1	2	3	4	5	6
k. SRU sit-in in law school Rotunda	1	2	3	4	5	6
l. Moratorium to discuss establishment of Univer-sity Senate	1	2	3	4	5	6
m. Occupation of Fayer-weather and Mathe-matics	1	2	3	4	5	6
n. Prevention of building takeover	1	2	3	4	5	6
o. PABPC sleep- and sit-in	1	2	3	4	5	6
p. Rally opposing recruit-ment by G.E. (Nov. 1969)	1	2	3	4	5	6
q. Hearings on nuclear reactor	1	2	3	4	5	6

20. Specify the campus organization and activities you were engaged in during the past year by circling the appropriate number after each activity.

	SRU	SDS	SCU	Other (please specify	Did not engage in
a. Signing petitions	1	2	3	_____	4
b. Writing leaflets	1	2	3	_____	4

	SRU	SDS	SCU	Other (please specify	Did not engage in
c. Passing out leaflets	1	2	3	_____	4
d. Manning tables	1	2	3	_____	4
e. Attending meetings	1	2	3	_____	4
f. Attending meetings					
As observer	1	2	3	_____	4
As member	1	2	3	_____	4

21. Have you worked for any student government committee since you have been at Columbia?

        1 No   2 Yes   (If yes, which _____)

22. Which of the following activities have you participated in during the past year? (Circle all that apply.)

a. Collection of signatures and funds for Biafran relief

b. Rallies and demonstrations in behalf of Israel

c. Loyalty day and other marches in support of soldiers in Vietnam

d. Anti-ABM meetings and demonstrations

e. Anti-Wallace demonstration (October 1966)

f. Pro-Teachers' Strike activities (1968)

g. Anti-Teacher's Strike activities (1968)

h. Demonstrations for Black Panthers

i. High school organizing

j. Picketing sellers of California grapes

k. Veteran's day parade and other activity in support of Nixon's Vietnam policy

l. Moratorium Day activities (October 15, 1969)

m. Moratorium activities (November 13 and 14, 1969)

n. November 15 march on Washington

o. Woodstock Festival

p. Work for political candidate (Name of candidate_____)

q. Letters to Congressmen, Mayor, etc. (Subject of letter[s] _____)

r. Other activities (please describe) _____
_____

23. Did you serve on committees which organized any of the above activities?

1 No   2 Yes   (If yes, which activities?_____
_____

24a. During the year before I came to Columbia the *two* strongest influences on my political beliefs were:

1 My family

2 My friends

3 My teachers

4 School-related reading

5 Newspapers and magazines

6 Participation in political activity

7 TV and radio

8 Other independent reading

24b. Since I have been at Columbia, the two strongest influences on my political beliefs have been:

1 My family	5 Newspapers and magazines
2 My friends	6 Participation in political activity
3 My teachers	7 TV and radio
4 School-related reading	8 Other independent reading

25. Was there any particular event during the past year which you feel deeply affected your political outlook?

    1 No   2 Yes   (If yes, please describe.)_____

26. If 10 represents the most *radical* student, 0 represents a *slightly liberal* student, and −10 represents a student who is very *conservative,* how would you rate yourself.

    −10 −9 −8 −7 −6 −5 −4 −3 −2 −1 0 1 2 3 4 5 6 7 8 9 10
    conservative   *liberal*   *radical*

    your closest friends (circle all numbers that apply)

    −10 −9 −8 −7 −6 −5 −4 −3 −2 −1 0 1 2 3 4 5 6 7 8 9 10

    your mother

    −10 −9 −8 −7 −6 −5 −4 −3 −2 −1 0 1 2 3 4 5 6 7 8 9 10

    your father

    −10 −9 −8 −7 −6 −5 −4 −3 −2 −1 0 1 2 3 4 5 6 7 8 9 10

Appendix D
Criteria for
Classifying Political Activity

I. All samples *except* high school sample, Yankelovich national sample, Columbia panel sophomores, and parents of Columbia panel.

Activitist: Reported participating in one or more of the following activities:

1. Demonstration or march for the civil rights or peace movements
2. Vietnam Summer
3. Draft counselling
4. Voter registration for civil rights
5. Two or more teach-ins on the Vietnam War
6. Organization of groups or protests in the civil rights or peace movements

Sympathizer: Reported doing any one of the following activities but not any of those listed under "activist":

1. Contributed money to civil rights or peace movements
2. Signed petitions for the civil rights or peace movements
3. Tutored underprivileged children
4. Attended one teach-in on the Vietnam War
5. Belonged to an organization supporting civil rights or peace movements

Nonactivist: Reported none of the above activities.

II. Columbia panel as sophomores. Respondents were divided into five groups on the basis of their reported political activity from the fall of 1968 to the fall of 1969.

Most radical: Reported participating in one or more of the following activities:

1. Demonstrations opposing the teacher's strike, New York City, 1968
2. Demonstrations in support of Black Panthers
3. Organizing for radical causes in the high schools
4. Working for radical political candidates

Activitist: Participated in the anti-Vietnam march in Washington, D. C., November 1968 but not in any of the activities listed under "most radical."

Concerned supporter: Participated in at least two of the following activities but not in any of those listed under "most radical" or "activist."

1. Collecting money and signatures for Biafran relief
2. Rallies in support of Israel
3. Anti-ABM meetings and demonstrations
4. Picketing sellers of California grapes in support of the farmworkers strike
5. Local anti-Vietnam marches and demonstrations
6. Working for liberal political candidates

Nonactivist: Participated in only one or none of the activities listed under "concerned supporter."

Conservative activist: Participated in at least one of the following:

1. Demonstrations in support of soldiers in Vietnam
2. Veteran's Day marches
3. Working for a conservative political candidate

Change scores in activity levels were calculated as follows:

1. If a student has been *nonactivist* upon entering Columbia, he was said to have:

   a. *Increased his activity* if as a sophomore he fell into one of the first three categories (most radical, activist, or concerned supporter)
   b. *Remained the same* (no change) if as a sophomore he was still a non-activist
   c. *Decreased his activity* (actually increased conservative activity) if as a sophomore he fell into the category conservative activist. (This group comprised only 6 students, 5 initially classified as nonactivist, 1 as sympathizer.)

2. If a student had been a *sympathizer* upon entering Columbia, he was said to have:

    a. *Increased his activity* if as a sophomore he fell into either of the first two categories (most radical or activist)

    b. *Remained the same* if as a sophomore he fell into the category concerned supporter

    c. *Decreased his activity* if as a sophomore he fell into either of the last two categories (nonactivisit or conservative activist)

3. If a student had been a *dissident activist* upon entering Columbia, he was said to have:

    a. *Increased his activity* if as a sophomore he fell into the first category (most radical)

    b. *Remained the same* if as a sophomore he fell into the second category (activist)

    c. *Decreased his activity* if as a sophomore he fell into either the third or four category (concerned supporters or nonactivist)

III. Yankelovich sample. A composite index was developed by weighting and summing the number of political activities in which a respondent reported participating. The weights used were as follows:

    Weight = 2: Sit-ins, riots, marches, civil rights protests

    Weight = 1: Political campaigns, organizational meetings of political groups

References

Abelson, R. P. Modes of resolution of belief dilemmas. *Journal of Conflict Resolution,* 1959, 3, 343-352.

Adorno, T. W., Frenkel-Brunswik, E., Levinson, D. J., & Sanford, R. N. *The authoritarian personality.* New York: Harper, 1950.

Astin, A. W. An empirical characterization of higher education. *Journal of Educational Psychology,* 1962, 53, 224-235.

Auger, C., Barton, A., & Maurice, R. The nature of the student movement and radical proposals for change at Columbia University. *The Human Factor,* 1969, 9 (1), 18-40.

Bachman, G. C. Youth looks at the future. Paper presented at the convention of the American Association for Public Opinion Research, Atlantic City, May 1972.

Barton, A. H. The Columbia crisis: Campus, Vietnam, and the ghetto. *Public Opinion Quarterly,* 1968, 32, 333-352.

Barton, A. H. *Support for campus demonstrators: Politics, peer group attitudes, and dissatisfaction.* Bureau of Applied Social Research Report, Columbia University, 1972.

Block, J. H., Haan, N., & Smith, M. B. Socialization correlates of student activism. *Journal of Social Issues,* 1969, 25, (4), 143-177.

Braungart, R. Family status, socialization, and student politics: A multivariate analysis. *American Journal of Sociology,* 1971, 77, 108-130.

Braungart, R. G. The sociology of generations and student politics: A comparison of the functionalist and generational unit models. *Journal of Social Issues,* 1974, 30 (2), 31-54.

Christie, R. Authoritarianism reexamined. In R. Christie & M. Jahoda (Eds.), *Studies in the scope and method of The Authoritarian Personality.* Glencoe, Illinois: Free Press, 1954.

Christie, R. Eysenck's treatment of the personality of communists. *Psychological Bulletin,* 1956, 53, 411-430. (a)

Christie, R. Some abuses of psychology. *Psychological Bulletin,* 1956, 53, 439-451. (b)

Christie, R. Relationships between Machiavellianism and measure of ability, opinion, and personality. In R. Christie & F. L. Geis (Eds.), *Studies in Machiavellianism.* New York: Academic Press, 1970. (a)

Christie, R. Scale construction. In R. Christie & F. L. Geis (Eds.), *Studies in Machiavellianism*. New York: Academic Press, 1970. (b)

Christie, R. Why Machiavelli? In R. Christie & F. L. Geis (Eds.), *Studies in Machiavellianism*. New York: Academic Press, 1970. (c)

Christie, R., & Cook, P. A guide to published literature relating to *The Authoritarian Personality* through 1956. *The Journal of Psychology*, 1958, **45**, 171-199.

Christie, R., & Garcia, J. Subcultural variations in authoritarian personality. *Journal of Abnormal and Social Psychology*, 1951, **46**, 457-469.

Christie, R., & Geis, F. Some consequences of taking Machiavelli seriously. In E. F. Borgatta & W. W. Lambert (Eds.), *Handbook of personality theory and research*. Chicago: Rand McNally, 1968.

Christie, R., & Geis, F. L. Implications and speculations. In R. Christie & F. L. Geis (Eds.), *Studies in Machiavellianism*. New York: Academic Press, 1970.

Christie, R., Havel, J., & Seidenberg, B. Is the *F*-scale irreversible? *Journal of Abnormal and Social Psychology*, 1958, **56**, 143-159.

Christie, R., & Lehmann, S. The structure of Machiavellian orientations. In R. Christie & F. L. Geis (Eds.), *Studies in Machiavellianism*. New York: Academic Press, 1970.

Connell, R. W. Political socialization in the American family: The evidence re-examined. *Public Opinion Quarterly*, 1972, **36**, 321-333.

Festinger, L. *A theory of cognitive dissonance*. Stanford: Stanford University Press, 1957.

Finney, H. C. Political libertarianism at Berkeley: An application of perspectives from the new student left. *Journal of Social Issues*, 1971, **27** (1), 35-61.

Flacks, R. The liberated generation: Explorations of the roots of student protest. *Journal of Social Issues*, 1967, **23**, (3), 52-75.

Geis, F. L., & Christie, R. Overview of experimental research. In R. Christie & F. L. Geis (Eds.), *Studies in Machiavellianism*. New York: Academic Press, 1970.

Geller, J. D., & Howard, G. Some sociopsychological characteristics of student protest activists. *Journal of Applied Social Psychology*, 1972, **2**, 114-137.

Gergen, K. J., & Gergen, M. M. Higher education: Missing in action. *Proceedings of the 78th Annual Convention of the American Psychological Association*, 1970, **5**, 880.

Grant, J. *Confrontation on campus: The Columbia pattern for the new protest*. New York: New American Library, 1969.

Greenstein, F. I. Personality and politics. In F. I. Greenstein & N. W. Polsby (Eds.), *Handbook of political science* (Vol. 2). Reading, Massachusetts: Addison-Wesley, 1975.

Jacobs, P., & Landau, S. *The new radicals: A report with documents*. New York: Random House, 1966.

Jones, E. E., & Nisbett, R. E. *The actor and the observer: Divergent perceptions of the causes of behavior*. New York: General Learning Press, 1971.

Kadushin, C. The friends and supporters of psychotherapy: On social circles in urban life. *American Sociological Review*, 1966, **31**, 786-802.

Keniston, K. *Young radicals: Notes on committed youth*. New York: Harcourt, Brace, & World, 1968.

Keniston, K. ACE study of campus unrest. *Science*, 1969, **165**, 1206-1207.

Keniston, K. *Radicals and militants: An annotated bibliography of empirical research on campus unrest*. Lexington, Massachusetts: Lexington Books, 1973.

Kerpelman, L. C. *Activists and nonactivists: A psychological study of American college students*. New York: Behavioral Publications, 1972.

Kunen, J. S. *The strawberry statement: Notes of a college revolutionary*. New York: Random House, 1968.

Lazarsfeld, P. S., Berelson, B., & Gaudet, H. *The people's choice* (3rd ed.). New York: Columbia University Press, 1968.

Lazarsfeld, P. S., & Merton, R. K. Friendship as social process: A substantive and methodological analysis. In M. Berger, T. Abel, & C. A. Page (Eds.), *Freedom and control in modern society.* New York: Van Nostrand, 1954.

Lewis, S. H., & Kraut, R. E. Correlates of student activism and ideology. *Journal of Social Issues,* 1972, **28** (4), 131-149.

Lipset, S. M., & Ladd, E. C., Jr. . . . And what professors think. *Psychology Today,* 1970, **4** (6), 49-51, 106.

Lipset, S. M., & Wohlin, S. S. *The Berkeley student revolt: Facts and interpretations.* Garden City, N.Y.: Doubleday, 1965.

McGuire, W. J. Inducing resistance to persuasion: Some contemporary approaches. In L. Berkowitz (Ed.), *Advances in experimental social psychology,* Vol. I, New York: Academic Press, 1964.

Mankoff, M., & Flacks, R. The changing social base of the American student movement. *Annals of the American Academy of Political and Social Sciences,* 1971, **395,** 54-67.

Mead, M. *Culture and commitment: A study of the generation gap.* Garden City, N.Y.: Doubleday, 1970.

Newcomb, T. M. *The acquaintance process.* New York: Holt, Rinehart, & Winston, 1961.

Newfield, J. *A prophetic minority.* New York: New American Library, 1966.

Pervin, L. A., & Rubin, D. B. Student dissatisfaction with college and the college drop-out: A transactional approach. *Journal of Social Psychology,* 1967, **72,** 285-295.

Sale, K. *SDS.* New York: Random House, 1973.

Somers, R. H. The mainsprings of rebellion: A survey of Berkeley students in November 1964. In S. M. Lipset & S. S. Wohlin (Eds.), *The Berkeley student rebellion: Facts and interpretations.* Garden City, N.Y.: Doubleday, 1965.

Thomas, L. E. Family correlates of student activism. *Developmental Psychology,* 1971, **4,** 206-214.

Warner, L. G., & DeFleur, M. L. Attitude as an interactional concept: Social constraint and social distance as intervening variables between attitude and action. *American Sociological Review,* 1969, **34,** 153-169.

Westby, D., & Braungart, R. B. Class and politics in the family background of student political activists. *American Sociological Review,* 1966, **31,** 690-692.

Yankelovich, D. What they believe: A Fortune survey. In *Youth in turmoil.* New York: Time-Life, 1969.

Yankelovich, D. *The changing values on campus: Political and personal attitudes of today's college students.* New York: Simon & Schuster, 1972.

Index

Numbers in italics refer to the pages on which complete references are listed.

A 6
B 7
C 8
D 9
E 0
F 1
G 2
H 3
I 4
J 5